Christianity and Pagan Culture in the Later Roman Empire

CHRISTIANITY AND
PAGAN CULTURE

IN THE LATER ROMAN EMPIRE

TOGETHER WITH

An English Translation of John Chrysostom's
*Address on Vainglory and the Right Way
for Parents to Bring Up Their Children*

†

BY M. L. W. LAISTNER

Cornell Paperbacks
Cornell University Press

ITHACA, NEW YORK

PREFACE

THE three chapters of this book were delivered as lectures at the University of Virginia on the James W. Richard Foundation, October 24–26, 1950. For several reasons it seemed appropriate to add as an Appendix my own version of John Chrysostom's address on education. It has never before been translated completely into English; it has a certain charm and interest of its own; and it throws light on one aspect of the subject discussed in the second chapter. Since this book went to press a microfilm of the Lesbos manuscript (see page 75) has come into my possession. The variants that it offers are few and trifling, so that no changes are called for in the English rendering which has been made from Schulte's text. A short article on this codex in due course will appear in *Vigiliae Christianae*.

It is a pleasure to express my appreciation of the honor extended to me by President Darden and the members of the Committee on Public Occasions of the University of Virginia in inviting me to give these lectures. I also desire to thank the Trustees of the Woodbrooke Settlement in Birmingham and Messrs. William Heffer and Sons, Cambridge, England, publishers of the *Woodbrooke Studies,* for gracious permission to quote two extended passages from the late Alphonse Mingana's translation of Theodore of Mopsuestia. Finally, I am most grateful to two good friends, Professor Harry Caplan of Cornell University and Professor Arthur Darby Nock of Harvard University, who read this book in manuscript and offered a number of valuable suggestions and criticisms.

M. L. W. LAISTNER

Ithaca, New York

CONTENTS

Christianity and Pagan Culture in the Later Roman Empire

Chapter I

PAGAN CULTURE

IN ITS DECLINE

THE UNIQUE interest of the long struggle between Christianity and paganism must be my excuse for venturing in three lectures to discuss some aspects of a subject about which a vast literature has accumulated since the days of Tillemont and Edward Gibbon. When the vitality of any historical topic is so enduring that it continues to attract the attention of inquirers for two centuries or more, there will be periodical changes in the broad interpretation of the recorded facts, since no two generations think exactly alike about the past. There will also be many changes in detail as new sources of information are from time to time revealed. These, when they are sufficiently numerous and significant, will in turn modify or correct older interpretations; or again, a hypothesis formulated in one age and rejected in the next, may be confirmed by fresh discoveries and its truth be re-established. Similarly, the accepted estimate of historical personages may call for drastic revision, as has happened lately with Theodore of Mopsuestia. The recovery of certain of his writings which were long believed lost makes possible a fairer judgment of the

[For notes to Chapter I, see pages 123–125.]

doctrines that he taught, so that his latest biographer, a distinguished Roman Catholic scholar, has vindicated him against the charge of heterodoxy which had led to the condemnation of Theodore's works one hundred and fifty years after his death.[1] Such changes and chances are familiar to every student of history. But, if his particular taste leads him to investigate the early centuries of Christianity, perhaps the most far-reaching revolution that the world has seen, he will encounter a special difficulty, that of maintaining an impartial temper when confronted at every stage of his inquiry not only by the ordinary controversies inseparable from the pursuit of knowledge, but too often by a bitter partisanship engendered by the religious background or affiliations of the authors, ancient and modern, whom he consults.[2] Happily the particular aspect of pagan and Christian antiquity with which these lectures will deal is uncontroversial, in the sense that it calls for no consideration of doctrinal questions; and therefore there will be no temptation to do otherwise than humbly to follow the instructions long since laid down by the historian of the *Decline and Fall:* [3]

It is the right, it is the duty of a critical historian to collect, to weigh, to select the opinions of his predecessors; and the more diligence he has exerted in the search, the more rationally he may hope to add some improvement to the stock of knowledge, the use of which has been common to all.

My topic, then, is a part of the history of education in the ancient world; my purpose, to contrast the old established pagan theory and practice with what may be called the perfect training of a Christian, and then to study in some of the Christian writers of the third and fourth centuries what was in effect a compromise. Christianity ultimately triumphed all along the line; but during the long contest between the old and the new its chief spokesmen, sometimes openly, sometimes with pardonable dissimulation, had gradually assimilated the methods and many of the ideas of Greek and Roman rhetoric and philosophy. Thus it was that a substantial heritage of antiquity passed both to Byzantium and to medieval Europe in the West.

One cannot rightly comprehend and appraise intellectual trends in any historic period without some understanding of the political, social, and economic background. Hence some brief remarks on the complex society of the later imperial age must precede and serve as an introduction to my main subject. There is no doubt that for the mass of the people material existence was hard. It is true that conditions during most of the fourth century were better than they had been in the third. After a prolonged period of civil war and unrest, which at times came perilously near to anarchy and which left no part of the empire untouched, a stable government had at last been established; and for a while the danger of invasion had been stayed. But Rome's neighbors in the North and in the East continued none the less to be a menace; and to ensure the security of the frontiers was one, and perhaps the most pressing, reason for the ruinous taxation imposed and maintained by Diocletian, Constantine, and their successors. The new fiscal system brought with it in turn the growth of a bureaucracy more numerous, but less efficient, than that which had sufficed in the age of the Antonines. It was accompanied, increasingly and relentlessly, by the principle of economic compulsion enforced with merciless vigor and even brutality, until virtually no class in the empire was immune. Predial serfdom, in fact if not immediately in name, became the rule on the land; in the towns close control over manual workers was exercised to prevent both change of trade and migration from their own to some other district where conditions might perhaps be better. Similar restrictions were imposed in the towns also on the upper class, whose members were responsible for the municipal government and on whom the burden of taxes pressed most heavily, because any shortage in the amounts assessed against each locality had to be made good out of their own pockets. The government was, in short, a harsh despotism. This, as it will always do, bred, on the one hand, evasion of the law, and, on the other, both official corruption and frequent miscarriage of justice, as can still be read in the sober pages of Ammian or deduced from the long series of ordinances preserved in the Theodosian Code.

Injustice and corruption in public life, grinding taxation, the extremes of wealth and poverty, so that for the mass of the people the conditions in which they lived and worked from day to day were at best uncertain, at worst engendered an all but hopeless despair—these were the material hardships that turned men to beliefs and cults which offered hope of an afterlife and of rewards and compensation for earthly suffering. Contrary to what has often been maintained, one can say that interest in religion, which showed itself in a multiplicity of ways, was more real and more widespread in the third and fourth centuries than at any other period of ancient

history. The number of pagan cults that attracted worshippers is bewildering; for, though the older cults of
Greece and Rome continued, new beliefs and rites had
spread westward from the Orient, and their appeal had
grown steadily more compelling. This process went on
in many forms and affected every class. Philosophical
systems ceased to be pure structures of human reason
and became modified by religious faith and mysticism.
The mystery cults, Greek and oriental, had many devotees. Gnosticism, of which the essential feature was
the belief that truth about God, man, and the universe
was attainable not by reason, but only through direct
revelation to, or illumination of, the individual, flourished
in many forms and numerous coteries.[4] Lower down the
scale came addiction to astrology and belief in the
efficacy of magic, divination, and other occult arts. Such
practices in their naked simplicity satisfied many, but
others combined them with some kind of pseudoreligious
or pseudophilosophical system.

The Christians for many a long year had been a despised
and often a persecuted sect, and it was not until the conversion of Constantine that their status became secure.
Yet at the time of the Edict of Toleration they still formed
a relatively small minority of the total population within
the empire. From A.D. 312 their progress was indeed
triumphant, but paganism and its cults showed remarkable tenacity, so that it would be a grave error to suppose
that these rapidly disappeared under the Christian emperors. It has been said that the senatorial class in Rome
and Italy was chiefly responsible for this survival.[5] No
one would deny that the senatorial families formed the
most homogeneous and best-organized group among the

upholders of the old regime, and their opposition to Christianity continued long after Julian's official but short-lived restoration of polytheism had collapsed ignominiously with his death. Nor were their efforts restricted to perpetuating the old state religion; they worked also for the better preservation of Rome's literary heritage. It is certainly no accident that the copying and editing of the Latin classics was carried on with great fervor by members of the senatorial aristocracy and by men of letters with whom they were in sympathy, during the later fourth and early fifth century.[6] Nevertheless, to single out the senatorial order in this way is to envisage only a part of the total view. It was perhaps not even the most important part; for it may well be asked whether one of the greatest obstacles that the Church had to overcome was not the loyalty with which the inhabitants of the provinces, and especially the rural population, clung to the older beliefs; and they did so irrespective of the local gentry. The evidence for this is abundant and unequivocal, consisting both of positive records that attest the continued celebration of various heathen rites and of the constant warnings uttered by Christian preachers, of which the following is a good example:

Service of Satan is everything dealing with paganism, not only the sacrifices and the worship of idols and all the ceremonies involved in their service, according to the ancient custom, but also the things that have their beginning in it. Service of Satan is clearly that a person should follow astrology and watch the positions and motions of the sun, the moon, and the stars for the purpose of travelling, going forth, or undertaking a given work, while believing that he is benefited or harmed by their motion or their course; and that one should believe the men who, after watching the motions of the stars, prognosticate by them. . . . Are service of Satan: the purifications, the washings, the knots, the hanging of yeast, the observances of the body, the fluttering or the voice of birds and any similar thing. . . . They called his glamour [i.e., Satan's], the theatre, the circus, the race-course, the contest of athletes, the water-organs and the dances, which the Devil introduced into this world under the pretext of amusement, and through which he leads the souls of men to perdition.[7]

Nevertheless such practices and beliefs continued and were still being denounced in the sixth century and later.[8]

The last sentence of the passage just quoted may serve to remind us that the secular government and the ecclesiastical authorities did not always see eye to eye. Life was not without its more cheerful aspects. The theater, the circus, the athletic and gladiatorial shows appealed to all classes of society and were deliberately fostered by the emperors and their representatives in order to keep the people reasonably contented with their lot. Immense sums were expended on these amusements both by the emperors and by their subordinates in the provinces, and John Chrysostom has left us a vivid picture of the enthusiasm with which the giver of some lavish entertainment was greeted by the spectators on his entry into the theater.[9] It would be easy to criticize successive Christian emperors who sanctioned spectacles which the leaders of the Church unanimously condemned. But not only was the proportion of pagans to Christians still great in the later fourth century, but many of the more easygoing Christians themselves were not disinclined to attend a show when occasion offered. Preachers like Chrysostom might thunder from their pulpits against popular amusements, especially when they took place on Sundays and kept members of the congregation away from church. But the government trod warily. First, on April 17, 392, circus games are prohibited on Sundays, except if the emperor's birthday falls on that day. Seven years later (August 27, 399) the instruction becomes more explicit: there shall be no theatrical performances, horse races, or any kind of spectacle on the Lord's day in any city, the emperor's birthday alone excepted. But even then the prohibition cannot have been strictly obeyed or enforced, for in 425 a third ordinance was passed which combined a restatement of the law with moral denunciation. After forbidding theaters, games, and races on Sundays in all the cities of the empire, the law continues: "If there be any even at this date who are held fast in the madness of Jewish impiety or the insane errors of brutish paganism, they must know that there is one time for supplications and another for pleasures." [10] But, though gladiatorial shows had been suppressed in 399, the other entertainments continued on weekdays as before. The reasons for the severely puritanical tone adopted by bishops and preachers are obvious—the close and old-standing association of such festivals with pagan cult, the brutality of gladiatorial and beast shows, and the low tone and even obscenity which characterized theater and mime.

But the antinomy between pagan culture and Christianity went much deeper, and clearly to understand it we must consider the character of education, and especially of higher education, during the later empire. In all essentials it was still the system which had been evolved in the fourth century B.C. in Athens and which had spread all over the Mediterranean world during the Hellenistic age. It consisted of three stages which corresponded very roughly with the division with which we are still familiar —elementary school, middle or high school, and finally college training. At the outset one is confronted with a question to which there is no certain answer. What was the proportion of literacy in the empire? It is probable that during the first and second centuries of our era the townsmen, or at least the great majority of them, could read and write; but, on the other hand, it seems unlikely that more than a small minority of the rural population was literate even in the age of Antonines. From the third century on, however, there was a decline in this as in so many other respects, and, as we shall see, those who were charged with the duty of preparing Christian converts for baptism were well aware that a certain percentage of their hearers would have to acquire the chief articles of the faith by oral repetition.[11] Early in the sixth century one preacher not only distinguishes between those members of his congregation who can, and those who cannot, read the Scriptures for themselves but tells us that he knows traders and shopkeepers who have to hire clerks to do their correspondence and keep their books for them.[12] But though there is, then, a good deal of uncertainty about the number of those who at any given period had had an elementary schooling, there is no doubt whatever that higher education was confined to a minority of those who, in an economic sense, were privileged. There is a revealing passage in Eusebius, in which it is related how a promising youth, who later studied theology and finally died a martyr, had previously had a complete training in the pagan schools. Eusebius adds a parenthesis which is part explanation, part apology, to the effect that the young man came from a wealthy family.[13] The benefits of a thorough education then, as already in the Hellenistic age, were reserved for a minority, and it was this minority which derived advantage from the libraries existing in many, if not most, of the larger cities; [14] for we must not make the mistake of assuming that these municipal collections of books resembled the modern free library either in size or purpose.

The most thoughtful of the ancient writers on higher education advocated a curriculum in which attention was paid to all the branches of human knowledge as then understood. But in practice this remained an ideal; higher education consisted in the intensive study of rhetoric, and those who were adequately versed in all the liberal arts were very few. The rhetors or sophists dominated the scene, and certainly there is no lack of liveliness in the picture that the varied sources present. Sophists were to be found in most of the larger cities, but the leading centers were Athens and Smyrna. In the fourth century we must add to these Antioch and Constantinople. There was keen competition among these professors when a chair endowed by imperial or at least municipal generosity fell vacant. Intrigues were not unknown, a circumstance that had been noted and duly satirized already in the second century by Lucian.[15] Successful teachers, like Scopelian at Smyrna, Prohaeresius in Athens, and Libanius in Antioch, attracted students from every quarter, a fact which helps to explain the constant attention paid in the classroom to correct diction and vocabulary. Many of the pupils came from outlying parts of the empire and spoke their local dialects of Greek, and the mother tongue of some who came from predominantly Semitic areas was not even Greek. If the teacher was popular or a man of established reputation, student partisanship was strong and did not stop short of kidnaping new arrivals, to ensure that these would not enroll in the classes of a rival.[16] There was also the familiar criticism of overpopular professors, whose students "leap about them like Bacchants about Dionysus," [17] and they were often accused by their enemies of being mercenary. Against this can be set the generosity of those who were willing to help the poor but promising boy.[18] The ordinary sophist who held no endowed chair, on the other hand, might have a hard time to make both ends meet.[19] Even the aged professor who was reluctant to resign and managed to hold on to the last was not unknown.[20]

In what did the training given by these men essentially consist? Their pupils, whose age at entrance seems to have varied considerably, though fifteen to sixteen was probably the normal, came to them after several years of schooling with a *grammaticus*. With him they would have read a good deal of poetry and drama and have become to some extent acquainted with prose literature. Though other authors, for example, the classical historians, were not neglected, the four writers who to the end of antiquity surpassed all others in popularity with the schoolmasters, if not with the boys, were Homer, Euripides, Menander, and Demosthenes. Memorization of extended passages from these classics was a most important part of the work; and it is significant that quotations or reminiscences from these four are much commoner in the writers of the Second Sophistic than citations from other authors. Grammar and syntax, reading aloud to teach a clear delivery and correct pronunciation, and the study of dialectal or archaic vocabulary all received careful attention. Nor was the subject matter neglected—the mythology in which Greek poetry abounds and the history of the past without which neither the historians nor the orators were intelligible. The pupils were also exercised frequently in composition of the simpler sort, and the best of the schoolmasters tried to teach them the first elements of literary criticism. Thus, by the time that at least the brighter or more diligent youths came to the rhetor, a reasonably good foundation had been laid for the more specialized education that he was expected to give them.

Insofar as the reading of literature and especially of oratorical prose continued, the curriculum of the rhetorical schools was a prolongation of the work begun with the *grammaticus*. Yet in the Greek-speaking East it would seem that the function of the schoolmaster was sharply distinguished from that of the sophist; in the West the *grammaticus* at times trenched on what was really the rhetor's department, a practice which Quintilian deplored.[21] The new material properly studied with the rhetor comprised rhetorical theory and its accurate application, for example, the five parts of oratory—invention, disposition, style, memory, and delivery; the five divisions of a correctly composed speech—introduction, statement of facts, proof, refutation, and conclusion; and the three kinds of style— the grand, the middle, and the simple. In determining which of these styles to employ, the student must learn to take into account the subject to be treated and the circumstances in which the oration was supposed to be delivered. Again, in each style certain defects must be carefully avoided: the grand in inexpert hands might easily become verbose, the simple degenerate into a bald triviality lacking any literary merit, the middle become nerveless and devoid of any distinctive quality. To attain perfection in each of these styles care must be taken in the choice of vocabulary, so that, on the one hand, colloquialisms, dialectal forms, and solecisms were avoided and, on the other, the words used were appropriate to the particular style. That there were practitioners of the art who allowed their foibles to get the better of them, so that their teaching was unsound in theory and in practice, we know from the satire of Lucian. It is in his pages that we meet not only the lover of bizarre and fancy words who is advised to go back to the best of the classical models, but also the eccentric professor whose pupil is told not to trouble his head about the ancients, to be pushful, brazen, and effeminate, and to interlard his speeches with obsolete turns of Attic diction.[22] A clear and harmonious arrangement of both words and subject matter was essential, together with a judicious and varied use of the figures of speech and the figures of thought.

Clearly the subject was one of great complexity, and a full course of study would last several years. Written exercises, graduated in difficulty according to their capacity, were required of the pupils at every stage; and the more careful instructors would, as far as possible, inquire into the special aptitude or deficiency of each boy entrusted to their care.[23] Recitation of the written themes, followed by discussion and criticism from the instructor and sometimes from fellow pupils, aided not only correct composition but correct delivery and gesture. Nor were competitions rare at which prizes were awarded to the best of the competitors. Indeed, already in Quintilian's time the frequency of these occasions had become something of an abuse against which he protested and—familiar note!—for which he laid the chief blame on the parents.[24] But these displays, like the solo performances of the sophists themselves, became even more popular after his time, and examples of such student declamations have been recovered from Egypt.[25] The most elaborate of these exercises were full-dress orations of either the deliberative or forensic type. The subject was sometimes taken from the Homeric saga; more often, however, the orator drew upon the great days of Athenian history. Sometimes the speeches were composed in direct imitation of classic prototypes— Socrates defending himself before his judges or Demosthenes counseling the Athenians to make war on Philip of Macedon. Sometimes, though the speaker and the general setting were historical, the attendant circumstances were, as far as we can now judge, invented. The expert sophist, indeed, prided himself on his skill in arguing both sides of a case with equal fluency and would strive to impart this difficult art to the best of his pupils. Thus, among the most famous discourses of Aristides were his five Leuctrian orations. Two of them presented the Theban and two the Lacedaemonian point of view in the summer of 371 B.C., while in the fifth the arguments for maintaining a strict neutrality were set forth. In the later imperial period, although popular taste preferred panegyrical or epideictic speeches, the other type was not wholly neglected, and there survive, for instance, two declamations by Libanius in which Neocles and Themistocles are imagined as arguing on opposite sides of a given case.[26]

It is easy to disparage higher education in the empire on the ground that it was narrow and that content was sacrificed to verbal dexterity. Yet several considerations should deter one from unqualified condemnation of the system. It is, for example, only too easy to judge the distant past in the light of our own experience, but the greater prominence allotted nowadays to science has come about quite recently. Even during the Hellenistic age, when the greatest scientific advances recorded in antiquity were made, it is doubtful that they often penetrated beyond a small group of specialists and reached a majority of the educated class. It is undoubtedly true that admiration for rhetoric and rhetorical displays went too far, and that a great part of what survives from the pagan literature composed in the imperial age was vapid and lacked originality. But is not the bulk of the literature produced in almost any age—and our own is assuredly no exception—ephemeral, admired one day and forgotten the next? Even the repetition of old themes and the adherence to long established art forms can be paralleled in other countries and times, where they have not been treated with the contempt or impatience that is reserved for the products of the Second Sophistic. Some of the more thoughtful or critical among the ancients were fully aware of the excesses to which the teaching of some sophists led. If, however, we regard the final stage of ancient education, as the best of the writers in antiquity judged it, as a means to an end, a fairer estimate of it becomes possible. All, from Isocrates to Quintilian and the pseudo-Plutarch, insist that the primary purpose of education must be moral training and condemn any system which ignores or slights the inculcation in the pupil of good principles of conduct. As a writer of the fourth century after Christ puts it: "We believe that a true education results, not in carefully acquired symmetry of phrases and language, but in a healthy state of mind, which has understanding and true opinions about things good and evil, honorable and base." [27] And what of its practical value? When he left the rhetor, the young man had a good knowledge of some at least of the great authors of the past; he had learned to express himself correctly and even elegantly in both speech and writing; and, concurrently, he had been trained to exchange ideas and maintain an argument with his fellows. In short, he had acquired some of the more valuable parts of what we still think of as a humane education. The underlying principles of the method are still as valid now as they were then, while its more specialized application survives in those countries where, as in Scotland and particularly in the United States, rhetoric or public speaking has long been an academic subject in its own right. An example culled from a volume of memoirs published in 1895 will illustrate this point. John Skelton draws an amusing picture of his student days and of W. E. Aytoun, the professor of Rhetoric and English literature in the University of Edinburgh:

Yet—a poet himself—he liked to encourage any spark of imagination there might be among us; and the weekly exercises he set us tried our metal. The Edinburgh rhetoric class-room in the 'forties and 'fifties might have been a school of the sophists. We were generally invited to write on some classical theme— Leonidas at Thermopylae, the speech of Aristides to the Athenian people, Dionysius and Damocles, Gladiators in the Roman arena, and such like. The worst was that the best of these imaginative diversions were generally read to the class; the honour was great no doubt, but it was somewhat trying to the nerves, as there was always a good deal of rather boisterous comment in the way of cheers and laughter, from a crowd of students.[28]

Finally, it was the best preparation for a career in the imperial service, which afforded employment to a very large proportion of the educated class. It was a valuable, indeed a necessary, preliminary to a legal career, and the lads who flocked to the chief law schools in the empire, to Rome, Berytus, or Constantinople, did so normally after they had completed their work in the school of the rhetor. Libanius alludes more than once to the spring exodus of students from Antioch to Berytus and to boats crowded with young men setting out for Rome. He and other writers also mention another indispensable requirement for Greek-speaking youths who chose the law or the civil service as a profession, namely, a good knowledge of Latin. A contemporary of Libanius, speaking of a proconsul of Greece who was equally at home in either language, fancifully compares the two tongues to two guardsmen (*doryphoroi*) who help him in his profession.[29]

But what, it may be asked, of science and philosophy? Broadly speaking one can say that, except perhaps in mathematics, new scientific discoveries are not recorded after *circa* A.D. 200. The best modern judges rate highly the attainments of Diophantus and Pappus, who belong to the third century, but the extent of their originality is far from clear. Diophantus' book on the solution of algebraic equations happens to be unique among mathematical treatises surviving from antiquity; but it may be based largely on the lost works of earlier scientists. A book, in short, may be of the greatest value *now* to historians of science, because so much else has perished, and yet be completely unoriginal. It is as a storehouse that Pappus' works are precious to the modern student. The very title of his chief book, *Collection,* suggests its character; for it is a commentary on the writings of earlier mathematicians and contains many quotations from them. We meet this title again in medicine. This science had reached its zenith with Galen, who died in 210. He had no successors as a scientific author, but one hundred and fifty years after his time Oribasius, at the request of the emperor Julian, assembled a great body of extracts from the medical literature of the past, and he called his compilation, *Medical Collections.* Greek astronomy culminates in Claudius Ptolemaeus; for, although he was in the main a compiler, he made some modest contributions of his own to the science, and among the mathematicians of antiquity his place is high. Certain of the Neoplatonists, inspired by the example of the founder of the Academy and influenced by Neopythagorean teaching, were serious students of mathematics. Two treatises by Iamblichus and a commentary on the first Book of Euclid by Proclus are still extant. None the less, scientific originality in the later empire had been superseded by a rigid traditionalism, the formulation of new discoveries or theories had yielded place to the laborious activity of the commentator and compiler. It is precisely the same general tendency that characterizes so much of the literature composed in the same period.

Although scientists might differ sharply among themselves, as we know on the authority of Galen was notably true in the rival schools of medicine, they do not appear to have been drawn into the educational controversies of the day. It was quite otherwise with the philosophers; for they stand out as the bitterest critics of the sophists and of their aims and methods. Historically this enmity takes us far back into the past, since it can be traced back ultimately to the rivalry between the schools of Plato and Isocrates in the fourth century B.C. But, even if it be granted with Burnet that the opposition between the curriculum of the Academy in Plato's time and the Isocratean program of education foreshadows what in more recent centuries has been described as the opposition between science and humanism, the difference between two educational ideals had already become blurred before the end of the Hellenistic age. Certainly during the whole imperial epoch the verbal onslaughts of philosophers on rhetoricians and of rhetoricians on philosophers have generally an air of artificiality; they sound like venerable commonplaces, though the change of heart experienced by Dion Chrysostom, who began as a sophist and ended up by preaching a creed compounded of Stoicism and the teaching of the Cynics, was doubtless genuine enough. Many of the philosophers themselves were careful to study the art which they affected to despise, and in Stoic practice the study of rhetoric formed a part of logic, one of the three broad divisions into which they, like other post-Aristotelian sects, divided their philosophical system. In any event, as extant writings show, both in method and expression the influence of the contemporary Sophistic on philosophy was profound.

The direct contribution of the philosophical schools

to the normal practice of higher education had also sensibly declined. In the Hellenistic age attendance at lectures given in one or more of the philosophic schools had been an obligatory, or at least a usual, feature of ephebic training at Athens and elsewhere; and Romans, like Cicero, who visited Greece to complete their education, divided their time between rhetoric and philosophy.[30] When, many years later, Cicero composed his treatise on the education of the orator, he, with his own experience in mind, still assigned a place of honor in his scheme to philosophic studies. But a comparison between his theory of education and Quintilian's reflects very clearly the changes that had come about in little more than a century. Quintilian also stresses the value of philosophy, but he is consciously echoing Cicero and attempting to rehabilitate in his own times the Ciceronian doctrine in opposition to the newer trends in education of which he strongly disapproved. Thus, while paying homage to a vanished ideal, he shows unmistakably that the commonly accepted practice of his day was different. This is not to say that philosophy had become the exclusive occupation of specialists; for there were always some men of letters, and even men of affairs, who received instruction in it in their youth. Epictetus, after he had settled in Nicopolis, had many hearers, and we owe most of what we know about him and his teaching to his pupil Arrian, an administrator and, in his later years, historian. Plutarch, as his *Moral Essays* prove, kept up the interest in Plato and the Stoics that had first been aroused in him in his student days; and Marcus Aurelius, whose principal philosophic guide had been Junius Rusticus, wrote his reflections on life and the Stoic ethics in his rare intervals of leisure or even on his military campaigns. Nevertheless, by the second century at latest, a course in philosophy was no longer the culminating experience of the majority of young men belonging to the privileged classes.

Acrid criticism was not reserved solely by the philosophers for the rhetoricians; they also attacked one another, and that at a time when the original doctrines of each school had been influenced and sometimes modified by the doctrines of its rivals. The result was what is generally termed eclecticism, the beginnings of which go back to the later second century B.C. Already Panaetius, though the most distinguished Stoic of his age, had admired both Plato and Aristotle. He was less of a rigorist than his predecessors and had even been affected by the skepticism of his contemporary, Carneades the Academic, so that neither his views on the physical universe nor his ethics conformed fully to those of the older Stoics.[31] Gradually the post-Aristotelian schools sank back more and more into traditionalism. They continued to teach the same set of tenets that had long been identified with their respective sects or else had been modified in some degree by the assimilation of doctrines taught by their rivals. Even among the Stoics it would be difficult to trace any new thought after the second century of our era. Still their influence continued to be strong; and it was not restricted to their pagan contemporaries but profoundly affected many Christian writers.[32] For the student of Christian literature and thought one aspect of the skepticism taught by the New Academy is also of importance. It appears to have been Carneades who, as a part of his negative attitude to the epistemology taught by other sects, inveighed against divination and particularly against astrologers whose doctrine of necessity he sought to controvert. His polemic was leveled primarily against the Stoics, the only one of the strictly philosophic schools to countenance or even to justify such beliefs.[33]

There was, however, one noteworthy exception to the general charge of intellectual stagnation which can be brought against philosophy from the later second century onward. That exception was Neoplatonism. It is one of the ironies of history that the man who is reputed to have taught the two most original minds of the third century, the pagan Plotinus and the Christian Origen, is himself little more than a name. Ammonius Sakkas left no writings of his own, and references to him in antiquity are very few. Hence it is hazardous to assume, though this has often been done, that Plotinus' system was directly inspired by the teaching of his master. Recent criticism, moreover, favors a solution of this problem of influence that, while it is more complex, is also more probable. Historically, as is now fully recognized, Neoplatonism is of great significance in the development of human thought, and that for several reasons. Although the differences between the post-Aristotelian schools, including the Platonic Academy in its later phases, had become less sharply defined, and individual philosophers, while they adhered officially to one sect, were in fact eclectic in their teaching, the bitter and often arid disputes between the schools continued without producing any strikingly new thought or doctrine. Neoplatonism, however, was an impressive attempt, by combining with the teaching of Plato elements derived from Aristotle and the Stoics and also from the Pythagoreans who, after a long period of obscurity had again emerged into greater prominence shortly before the beginning of the Christian era, to create a systematic body of ideas which would still conform to the Greek philosophical tradition and at the same time would more effectively combat the enemy without. Its opponents were, on the one side, various Gnostic groups and the devotees of the mystery religions, and, on the other, at least after Plotinus' own time, the Christians. Thus Plotinus' precise relation to Ammonius Sakkas, though an interesting point in itself, is historically of minor significance, because many of the trends which helped to form his thinking and enabled him ultimately to evolve a new doctrine were far older. In the second place, Plotinus returned to those problems of metaphysics which had long been avoided or slighted in the schools. How can man or the human soul be brought into closer relation with the divine Creator of the universe? How is it possible to reconcile belief in an omnipotent and benevolent Deity with the existence of evil in the world? How disprove that the physical universe operates under a law of blind necessity? These were no idle academic questions; for both the Manichaeans and the Gnostic sects regarded all matter as evil and taught the existence of a malignant or destructive power in constant conflict with the divine Creator. Plotinus' system strove to combine with the traditionally Greek effort to solve these questions by the use of human reason a means of salvation for the individual. This was promised by religions and creeds which, whatever their merits or demerits, transcended man's understanding and relied for their appeal and their effect not on the exercise of reason but on an act of faith. Plotinus' system, in short, was an attempt to reconcile a mystical intuition of God with a rationalistic explanation of the physical universe. The successors of Plotinus, especially Iamblichus, went far beyond the doctrines and intention of their master. Still, in spite of their extravagances in the direction of what would nowadays be called spiritualism and theosophy, Neoplatonism had a long life; [34] and it is legitimate to wonder whether it would have exerted so wide an influence or the school itself have survived to the age of Justinian, if its leaders had been content only to propagate the austere philosophy of Plotinus himself.

It was long the fashion to explain the decline and fall of the Roman empire as the result of one main trend or one set of factors, political, economic, social, or religious; indeed, this convenient method of writing history is perhaps not extinct even now. The foregoing sketch, however imperfect, of society and education in the later imperial age will at least serve as a general reminder that such simplification of the past is inadmissible; and that the particular phenomenon which has emerged from this brief survey is the persistence in a complex society, heterogeneous in race, customs, and traditions, of a stable and old-established culture. The material civilization passed away, but the intellectual achievement of Greece and Rome did not perish. In a new and wholly Christian world the pagan or classical heritage, precariously at first, then with ever-growing vigor, lived on.

Chapter II

THE TRAINING OF THE

CHRISTIAN CONVERT

THE EDUCATIONAL system of the Graeco-Roman world which, as we have seen, exhibits a remarkably uniform character, was acceptable to all save two groups within the empire, the Jews and the Christians. The Jewish communities of Palestine and the Dispersion continued their traditional methods of instruction in or connected with the synagogue. Individual scholars, of whom the most eminent was Philo, studied pagan philosophy with the purpose of bringing its tenets into harmony with Jewish beliefs. There were also some Jews who became hellenized so completely that they ceased to be acceptable to their coreligionists; but there is no reason to believe that these extremists ever formed more than a small minority of the whole body of Jewry. Although the Roman authorities very soon had learned to distinguish Christians from Jews, and the very name, *Christianus,* may have had for them almost from the beginning a political rather than a religious connotation, the generality of pagans continued to regard the Christians as a dissident Jewish sect.[1] Thus, at the beginning of the second century so intelli-

[For notes to Chapter II, see pages 125–129.]

gent an observer as Epictetus at one time refers to Jews, when the context shows that he has Christians in mind, at another time he alludes to them as a separate group whom he calls Galilaeans. Some fifty years later Aristides in his *Apology* adopts an air of qualified friendliness to Judaism which contrasts strongly with the hostility of Christian writers in the next generation.[2] By what date was the break between Judaism and Christianity, which was signalized by an overt anti-Jewish polemic, complete? The answer usually given to this question has recently been well expressed by one critic who remarks: "However strong the Jewish influence which still might be exerted upon Christian thought and polity by its origins and by the retention of the Jewish Scriptures as 'inspired,' after A.D. 70 there are no more direct contacts with contemporary Judaism save hostile ones."[3] But the evidence hardly warrants the assumption that the Jewish wars of Vespasian and Titus were a decisive event for the relations between these two religious groups; it points rather to the conclusion that the open enmity of Christians to Jews dates from the suppression of the last insurrection against Roman authority in Judaea during the later years of Hadrian.[4]

The familiar assertion that the early Christians were recruited exclusively from the poorest section of the free population and from slaves is neither likely nor provable. Certainly by the beginning of the second century there were already many converts who enjoyed at least a moderate competence; for this can be deduced from documents which enjoin fasting on several days in the week in order that the food so saved may be given to the destitute and to widows and orphans: "And if there is among them a man that is poor and needy, and they have not an abundance of necessaries, they fast two or three days that they may supply the needy with the necessary food." [5] Even as late as the third century Christians were warned against accepting alms or pecuniary help from heathen sinners of all kinds.[6] Again, when the Scriptures were translated into Latin, the unknown translators used the language of everyday speech (*sermo plebeius*), not the literary idiom of the age, which many of the congregation would have found difficult to understand. This proves that a great proportion of churchgoers at that time were simple folk with little formal education. Pagan readers of these early Latin versions were repelled by what they affected to regard as their crudity.[7] Nevertheless, it was these Christian congregations in the West, or at least some of their members, who were largely responsible for enriching the Latin language; for gradually a specifically Christian Latin was developed, partly by taking over loan words from Greek and Hebrew, partly by attaching new meanings to many older words, partly by the creation of neologisms.[8]

But if there is necessarily much uncertainty about the economic status of the Christians for at least a century after the Crucifixion, there is none about their social and political disabilities, so long as they belonged to a sect that, *qua* sect, had been officially designated as "illicit" at least since the time of Trajan, and that at times suffered persecution. They were debarred from public office and from careers in the imperial or even the municipal services, since these involved some participation in the cult of the emperor, if in no other pagan rites. This was, and seems to have remained, the legal position; but in practice, as time went on, the law might become a dead letter. Active persecution fell into abeyance for considerable periods; when it did occur it was localized in a particular area and resulted from mob prejudice and violence which forced the imperial authority there to intervene. We also find in certain Christian authors and documents strict injunctions to the faithful to keep to themselves and to shun occupations and professions which would compel them regularly to associate with their pagan fellows. Yet it is certain, especially from the epigraphic evidence, that from the later second century Christians were to be found in some areas, for example, in Asia Minor and in Spain, holding municipal office.[9] In short, among the leaders of the Christian communities there were two schools of thought, the one rigorist, the other more farsighted, because they rightly believed that any *modus vivendi* which despite the law existed between the Christians and their gentile neighbors, so long as it endured, must favor the spread of the true faith. The situation changed greatly for the worse during the sixty years between Decius and Constantine; for, although only some of the emperors took active measures against the Christians, those that did so instigated a general persecution throughout the empire with the deliberate intention of destroying all who refused to recant. These efforts to uproot Christianity failed; and, while many of the weaker brethren relapsed under the threat of torture and death, the Christian communities as a whole triumphantly survived the test, which finally ended when Constantine adopted a policy of toleration. His own conversion, moreover, made Christianity the official religion of the imperial house.

Most of the surviving literature composed before *circa*
A.D. 200 has come down to us anonymously; or, if a name
has been attached to a particular work, it is either
demonstrably false or else meaningless, because nothing is known of the author. Again, there are some, like
Ignatius, who are historical personalities but of whose
youth and training no record exists, and this is often true
even after the second century. There remain those about
whom some reliable biographical information is to be
found either in their own works or elsewhere. Almost all
were adult converts: men who before they became Christians had been exposed to the normal educational curriculum of the Graeco-Roman world. It is thus exceedingly
difficult to assess the average level of education among
the rank and file; but then, as we have seen, owing 'to
the same paucity of evidence any inquiry into the literacy
of their gentile contemporaries is also doomed to failure.
In the earlier period even the bishop might be a man with
little formal education; from the time of Constantine
this can have happened rarely, if ever.[10] Among the ordinary converts, however, there were always some, especially
in rural areas, who could not read and write and therefore
had to be taught the essential articles of the faith orally:

For since all cannot read the Scriptures, some being hindered
as to the knowledge of them by want of learning, and others by
want of leisure, in order that the soul may not perish from ignorance, we comprise the whole doctrine of the faith in a few
lines. . . . So for the present listen while I simply say the
Creed, and commit it to memory.

So spoke Cyril of Jerusalem in 348. A generation later
Niceta of Remesiana addressed his baptismal candidates

in the simplest language possible and impressed on them the need of memorizing the Creed and Lord's Prayer. The pieces that the catechumen had been taught in this way in one week he was expected to repeat in the next.[11]

What were the provisions for specific instruction in Christian doctrine, first, to children of Christians and, secondly, to converts? Again for the earliest period information is sparse. The duty of Christian parents to bring up their children rightly had been laid down by St. Paul in his letter to the Ephesians (6:1–4).[12] It is therefore surprising that the orthodox Fathers, with the exception of John Chrysostom who delivered a homily on this text, do not in connection with this passage in the New Testament enlarge on the controversial aspects of Christian education. Only the heresiarch Pelagius comments quaintly on the words, "provoke not your children to wrath." They can be interpreted in two ways: parents may provoke their children's anger by whipping them immoderately or unreasonably or else by urging them on to secular studies and causing them thus to become acquainted with wrath.[13] The post-Pauline documents are explicit: "Thou shalt not withhold thy hand from thy son and thy daughter, but thou shalt teach them the fear of God from their youth up." [14] Adults must set a good example to the young, and in that very early sermon, wrongly called the *Second Epistle of Clement,* we read: "As a reward I beg of you to repent with all your heart and give to yourselves salvation and life. For if we do this, we shall set a mark for all the young who wish to work in the cause of piety and the goodness of God." [15] But the fullest instruction of this kind is of much later date, although the basic material is earlier. In the *Apos-*

tolic Constitutions the obligations of parents with children to rear are set out in no uncertain terms:

Fathers rear your children in the Lord, bringing them up in the nurture and admonition of the Lord (Ephesians 6, 4), and teach them arts that are serviceable and befitting this Word, that they may not, waxing wanton through prosperity and remaining unpunished by their parents, find license unseasonably and rebel against the good. Therefore do not hesitate to reprove them, chastening them with severity; for by correction you will not slay them, but rather will save them, as Solomon says in his Wisdom (Proverbs 29, 17): "Correct thy son and he shall give thee rest; even so shall he fill thee with good hope." "Thou shalt beat him with the rod and deliver his soul from death" (*ib.* 25, 14). And again the same sayeth thus (*ib.* 13, 24): "He that spareth his rod hateth his son"; and again we read (Ecclesiasticus 30, 12): "Smite his loins sore while he is little, lest he become stubborn and rebel against thee." So he who forbears to exhort and chasten his son, hateth his own child. Teach your children the word of the Lord, straiten them even with stripes and render them submissive, teaching them from infancy the Holy Scriptures, transmitting to them your words and God's words and all the divine writings; not permitting them to exercise authority over you against your judgment, nor allowing them to foregather for carousal with their equals in age; for in that way they will be diverted into disorder and fall into fornication. And if they suffer this by their parents' heedlessness, those that begat them shall be responsible for their souls. If the children, by reason of their parents' sloth, consort with licentious men, though they have sinned, they alone will not be punished, but their parents shall be brought to judgment on their behalf. Therefore give heed that you contract betimes to join them in wedlock, that in the burning heat of youth habits of fornication may not ensue, and you shall be held to account by the Lord God on the Day of Judgment.[16]

Provision for the proper instruction of the convert must have been made from the very beginning in the Christian communities. As they grew, the organization of the Church was perfected, a process that was already well under way when the *Pastoral Epistles* were composed.[17] The faithful were under the care of a regular clergy; religious instruction of children may have been carried on in part by them, to supplement parental teaching. The opening sections of the *Didache* consist of a brief set of exhortations to the Christian life. In the main they are prohibitive, an elaboration of the Decalogue interspersed with admonitions derived from the Gospels.[18] Similarly, what remains of Clement of Alexandria's address to the newly baptized is a plea to his hearers to practice self-control and courtesy to others on all occasions and to face adversity with a cheerful heart.[19] The tone of this sermon (*circa* 200) reflects a time when the Christians from necessity still kept much to themselves. If they conducted themselves as Clement would have them do, they would be a living proof that the accusations and prejudices of their gentile contemporaries were untrue.

It is in this period also that the sources begin to throw light on the important matter of catechetical instruction. There were two phases of this. The Christian communities were made up of those who had been baptized and who alone were full members of the congregation and of those who were still probationers and excluded from participation in the Eucharist until after their baptism. But before the non-Christian could even be admitted to the probationary class, he must give certain undertakings and receive some elementary teaching in the faith.

Certain occupations—prostitution, play-acting, the professions of charioteer or gladiator, of magician or astrologer—were forbidden to the convert and must be abjured before he could be admitted to instruction. According to one rigoristic document pagan schoolmasters are to give up their calling unless they have no other means of livelihood; once they are themselves adequately prepared, they might put their experience as teachers to use by becoming catechists.[20]

To what extent the baptism of infants or even of small children was customary in the early Church is a problem of some obscurity. Although Origen stated that the Church had received the tradition from the Apostles to baptize even the very young (*parvulis*), the practice is not clearly attested before the close of the second century.[21] As it continued for another two hundred years to be a matter for dispute, it clearly was not generally followed. Tertullian in an early work (*circa* 198–200) advocates delaying baptism until adolescence, so that the candidate may be old enough fully to understand the grave step that he is taking. Cyprian speaks of infant baptism without disapproval but does not urge it; his attitude seems to have been similar to that of Origen. Gregory of Nazianzus, a century after Cyprian, does not rule out the practice but would wait until the child is three years old, more or less, and has some rational understanding; but it may be questioned whether this obvious but not very satisfactory compromise can have commended itself to many.[22] The truth is that much the greater proportion of new Christians were converts; furthermore, baptism was a very solemn act which called for a long period of preparation, and putting off this sacrament until manhood or even until late in life was customary even when both parents of a candidate were Christians. Gregory of Nazianzus himself was not baptized until he had completed his education and was nearing thirty years of age, in fact not until shortly before his ordination. The postponement of the rite until just before death—the most famous instance is that of Constantine—cannot have been rare. John Chrysostom deplores such laxity in an eloquent passage in which he contrasts the joy surrounding the baptism of those who receive this sacrament when in their full vigor with the gloomy and depressing circumstances that mark repentance and baptism on the deathbed.[23] The reason for delay was that baptism ensured to the repentant catechumen forgiveness for past sins. But, unlike certain pagan ceremonies, such as the *taurobolium,* which was believed to bring about the "rebirth" of the worshipper for a term of years and which could be renewed, baptism could not be repeated.[24] Hence the Fathers are careful to warn those about to be baptized against the mortal danger of relapsing into sin. In the words of Chrysostom, "Baptism can give remission of former sins. But the fear is not slight, the peril is not trifling, that some time we return again to sin and that the healing drug turns to festering poison. The greater the Grace that we have received, the heavier the punishment for those who sin after baptism." [25] The baptism of infants, in short, did not become the rule until the fifth century, and in general it is ignored in the extant catechetical literature.[26] But by then the number of adult converts had dwindled greatly, and the importance of the catechumenate had correspondingly declined. It is likely that the Augustinian teaching on the doctrine of original sin had greatly contributed to bring about this change. Certainly he is the one writer who urged infant baptism with steady persistence.[27]

Apart from general exhortations to parents to bring up their children in the Christian way of life, most writers have little to say about the religious training of the young. Two letters of Jerome are indeed of great interest to historians of education; but the little girls on whose education from birth he advises their parents were both intended for the conventual life. John Chrysostom's address entitled, *On Vainglory and the Right Way for Parents to Bring Up Their Children*,[28] supplemented by many shorter passages in his homilies, is therefore of peculiar value; for the boys and, incidentally, the girls whom he had in mind were the children of the laity who, like their parents, would marry and enter on various civil occupations. One wonders how far his advice was adopted in Christian households at Antioch or elsewhere. The central portion of the tract is especially worthy of attention; for in it he sketches a catechetical method adapted to young minds. Basing his system on psychological factors, he would exploit to the full that love for stories which is characteristic of all normal children, as well as their inquisitiveness and love of emulation. He takes two episodes from the Old Testament and shows how these can be told to the child, partly in the actual words of the Bible, partly in simpler language where the text of the Septuagint is too prolix for a youthful intelligence. Having explained and illustrated his method, he leaves it to the parents to apply it in a similar way to other parts of the Old Testament story. The New Testament is left until a boy is older; for even the narrative portions are more than a tale from which an improving moral can be pointed. They necessarily involve some of the fundamentals of Christian belief which, however simply stated, demand a maturer understanding.

Many of Augustine's shorter treatises were composed in answer to specific requests made to him by correspondents who desired guidance on points of doctrine or cult. Thus his short tractate *On Catechising the Uninstructed* was the practical reply to an inquiry addressed to him by Deogratias, a deacon of the Church in Carthage. It differs from other surviving catechetical works because it is concerned not with catechumens preparing for baptism but with non-Christians who were seeking admission as probationers, that is, into the lower grade of catechumens; for it would seem that, at least from the time of Constantine, when conversions became far more numerous than they had been before, a more elaborate procedure developed. Where before there was but one body of catechumens, they were now divided into two classes or grades; the lower comprised the ordinary converts, the upper those who had signified their intention to be baptized and who received special instruction all through Lent so that their baptism could take place at Eastertide.[29] Augustine's treatise was written to meet a local need, but it soon became more widely known because of its excellence and the fame of its author. It falls into two parts. The first lays down instructions for the catechist about what he has to teach and on what plan he should proceed. Augustine points out that there are three types of convert with whom Deogratias may have to deal: the uneducated and illiterate (*idiotae*),[30] those who had received the normal pagan schooling in the classes of the *grammaticus* and *rhetor,* and, finally, those who were highly cultured. These last, who were likely to have some acquaintance already with Christian literature, should be encouraged to persevere in their reading; if they had encountered heretical books, they must be instructed and discreetly warned. The applicants of the second class must be exhorted not to give themselves airs because of their literary education. They should be urged to study the Scriptures written in plain and unadorned language and told not to sneer at preachers who were guilty of solecisms and barbarisms in their speech or who read badly. In this contrast between two types of educated person one can detect an echo of the old rivalry between rhetoric and philosophy. The man of true culture will not preen himself on his attainments; the typical product of the sophistic schools will. Truly, the prospective converts comprised "all sorts and conditions of men," and the task of the catechist was not easy. As Augustine tells Deogratias:

But as we are now discussing the teaching of candidates, I can assure you from my own experience of my varied reactions to those whom I see before me waiting to be instructed. He may be educated or slow-witted, a citizen or a stranger, a rich man or a poor man, one who has held no public office or one who has, a man wielding some authority, a person of this or that family, of this or that age or sex, coming to us from this or that (philosophical) sect or from this or that popular error; and the divers ways in which they affect me determine the manner in which my lecture begins, continues, and ends.[31]

In the second half of the treatise Augustine introduces a specimen of a catechetical address suitable for an educated townsman; for Deogratias would have many such to instruct. He begins by warning his hearer against those who wish only for pleasure or wealth, against false Christians who look only to temporal advantage, and still others who become fainthearted if they see some of their fellows more prosperous than themselves. Then he passes on to the main section of the address, dwelling on God and His work of Creation, and summarizing the chief stages of the Old Testament story—the Old Covenant. Chronologically this is equivalent to five ages, the fifth extending from the Babylonian Captivity of the Jews to the birth of Christ. Next he comes to the sixth age, that is to say, Christ's earthly life and Passion, the missionary labors of St. Paul, and the spread of Christianity after the death of the Apostle, first in a persecuted Church and finally in its last phase since Constantine. The address ends with a general exhortation to the would-be catechumen to be steadfast in the faith, to trust in God, and to withstand the temptations of the flesh that he sees all about him. The treatise itself concludes with a specimen of a shorter address in which the survey of the six ages is omitted.

For many years the length of time that must elapse between conversion and full membership of the congregation after baptism, though never short, had varied greatly. In A.D. 305 the Synod of Elvira fixed a minimum of two years' preparation for baptism but allowed a shorter probation for sick persons. Three years is the requirement in the *Canons of Hippolytus,* but the time might be reduced if a pupil proved himself exceptionally zealous and apt, and these also are the provisions laid down in the *Apostolic Constitutions.*[32] One writer sets the probationary term at "not less than six years," but this, in view of the other evidence, cannot refer to the normal requirement but must reflect his own notions on the subject.[33] When the practice of distinguishing a lower from a higher order of cate- chumens became established, the preparation of those who were to be baptized became much briefer. The lower class would be familiar in outline with the religion which they had embraced and with those parts of the divine service which they were permitted to attend. It remained only to give to the candidates for baptism a relatively short but intensive course of instruction which, as we have seen, was normally carried on through the Lenten season. Ordinarily the preparation of these persons had always been entrusted to a priest or deacon, but at least down to the end of the third century laymen had sometimes acted as catechists, provided that they were qualified for this responsibility by their knowledge and grave character. A probable example of this was Origen before his ordination *circa* 230, and it is possible that both Clement of Alexandria and Tertullian were laymen.[34] The catechumen, before he was ready for baptism, must have received instruction on certain basic aspects of Christian doctrine: the nature of God and the Trinity; the creation and order of the universe; the purpose of the creation of the world and man's place in it; man's human nature; God's punishments for the wicked and rewards for the saints, and His mercy to mankind. Finally, after a prayer by bishop or priest, the catechist expounded the meaning of the Incarnation, Passion, Resurrection, and Assumption of Christ.[35]

More revealing and more vivid than Church ordinances are the extant allocutions to baptismal candidates, supple- mented by the graphic narrative of Aetheria. Indeed, we are unusually well informed about the procedure in Pales-

tine and Syria during the fourth century. In spite of minor
variations, it exhibits a uniformity that had been slowly at-
tained during a long antecedent period. The primary purpose of the addresses was to teach the articles of the faith,
but they also contain as a recurrent feature passages con-
demning and warning against Judaism, pagan rites and
superstitions, and heresies, particularly those that were rife
at the time when the allocutions were delivered. Aetheria,
who made a pilgrimage from Spanish Galicia to Palestine
between the years 415 and 417, describes how those wish-
ing to be prepared for baptism were required to hand their
names in to the priest at the beginning of Lent.[36] Subsequently the male applicants had to appear before the
bishop accompanied by their fathers, the female by their
mothers. They then had to affirm to him that they were "of
good life," obedient to their parents, sober, and serious-
minded. Any candidate whose answers or credentials were
unsatisfactory was told to depart and amend his way of life
before returning. Strangers, unless they brought sufficient
references from their home country, were not readily admitted. The preparation of the candidates continued
through Lent. An interesting sidelight is thrown by
Aetheria on the language difficulty. As some of the population spoke Aramaic and some spoke Greek, the bishop's
addresses, which were always in Greek, were translated
into Aramaic by an interpreter. Persons from the West who
understood neither of these languages were aided by
Greek-speaking monks or nuns who were familiar with
Latin. It was in this same diocese of Jerusalem that Bishop
Cyril in 348 delivered a series of sermons to a mixed group
of candidates for baptism, some being persons of good edu-

cation, others clearly not; for in his fourth sermon, before expounding certain Christian dogmas, he observes:

Let those here present whose habit of mind is mature and who "have their senses already exercised to discern good and evil" (Hebrews 5, 14) endure patiently to listen to things fitted rather for children, and to an introductory course, as it were, of milk: that at the same time both those who have need of the instruction may be benefited, and those who have the knowledge may rekindle the remembrance of things which they already know.

Similarly, in a later address he says: "But lest any from lack of learning should suppose from the different titles of the Holy Spirit that there are divers spirits, and not one and the self-same, which alone there is . . ." [37] Cyril's course of instruction is in its way a model. It is well arranged, the thought is lucidly expressed, and the language is simple yet lively. After two sermons of an introductory character he begins his exposition proper by discoursing on repentance and remission of sins, to ensure that his auditors are in a suitable frame of mind for what is to follow. Next he explains the meaning and purpose of baptism and then passes on to essential belief concerning the Godhead, together with practical admonitions about fasting, dress, and the reading of Scripture. The fifth address has as its subject faith, the sixth the unity of the Godhead, and at this point Cyril takes occasion to warn his hearers against contemporary heresies. They are now ready to be instructed in the articles of the faith, and so in twelve addresses he explains in some detail each phrase of the Creed. Orthodox in doctrine, it differs only in some minor points from the Nicene formula. The eighteen addresses form a coherent series of

prebaptismal sermons. But there are five others that have
commonly been assigned to Cyril but that are more probably the work of John, his successor in the see of Jerusalem.[38] Since they were intended for those who had just
been baptized and thereby had become full members of
the Christian congregation, they expound sacramental
doctrine; and there is also a brief explanation, sentence by
sentence, of the Lord's prayer.

The method of catechetical instruction in Antioch and
neighboring bishoprics during the fourth century can now
be illustrated not only from two addresses by John Chrysostom, but more particularly from a series of sixteen short
allocutions by Theodore of Mopsuestia. Although manuscripts of the Greek original were destroyed when the
Council of Constantinople in 553 pronounced the formal
condemnation of Theodore and his works, an early Syriac
version survived. This was discovered and first published
by the late Alphonse Mingana who, with full justice, described the hitherto lost commentary on the Nicene Creed
as "one of the most important theological works of the
golden age of Christianity." [39] Theodore explained the
Creed in ten addresses; of the remaining six one deals with
the Lord's prayer, three deal with baptism, and two with
the Eucharist. Like Cyril he has the gift of handling a difficult subject in clear and simple language. He further tries
to help the understanding of the catechumens, some of
whom were no doubt craftsmen working in the city while
others came from the countryside near Mopsuestia in the
province of Cilicia and not far from the Syrian border, by
introducing similes drawn from everyday life. The religious
ceremonies of pagans are like the make-believe of a play in

the theater. The regeneration of a Christian is like refashioning of damaged pottery. Every body has its shadow, but we cannot identify the shadow alone. The newly baptized is like an infant in swaddling clothes. There are the usual warnings against various heretical sects, particularly the followers of Arius, and against Judaism and Judaizers in the Christian community. The baptismal candidate approaching the priest suggests to the catechist an elaborate comparison, as follows:

When a person wishes to enter the house of a man of power in this world, with the intention of doing some work in it, he does not go direct to the master of the house and make his engagement and contract with him—as it is unbecoming to the master of the house to condescend to such a conversation—but goes to the majordomo and agrees with him about his work, and through him agrees with the master of the house, to whom the house and all its contents belong. In this same way you act, you who draw nigh unto the house of God, which is the Church of the living God, as the blessed Paul says (I Timothy 3, 15), because God is as much greater than we are as He is higher in His nature than we are, and is for ever invisible and dwells in a light which is ineffable, according to the words of the blessed Paul (*ib*. 6, 16). We approach, therefore, the majordomo of this house, that is to say, of the Church, and this majordomo is the priest, who has been found worthy to preside over the Church; and after we have recited our profession of faith before him, we make with God, through him, our contract and our engagements concerning the faith, and we solemnly declare that we will keep His love always and without a change. After we have, by our profession of faith, made our contracts and engagements with God our Lord, through the intermediary of the priest, we become worthy to enter His house and enjoy its sight, its knowledge and its habitation, and to be also enrolled in the city and its citizenship. We then become the owners of a great confidence.[40]

Two extant homilies by John Chrysostom are very characteristic of him. Save for some remarks on the significance of the baptismal rite itself, he dwells not on doctrine, but on the conduct that should distinguish those whom he is addressing. They are, in short, general exhortations suited to the particular occasion, his hearers doubtless receiving at other times their formal instruction in the articles of the faith.[41] He counsels them earnestly against swearing and the taking of oaths, against the theater and the circus, against ostentatious dress (especially on the part of female converts), and against superstitious practices, like the belief in omens and the wearing of amulets. His admonitions, as usual, are enlivened by graphic similes. God cleanses the contrite soul as men clean a statue which has become discolored by age, smoke, and grime. Chrysostom draws a parallel from the athletic festivals and describes the painter who carefully outlines his figures, when they can still be altered or erased, before applying the colors which cannot so easily be changed.

The *Great Catechism* by Gregory of Nyssa is in a class by itself, being composed not for catechumens but for their instructors; at the same time it is clear that the converts whom he has in mind and whom his readers will have to prepare are persons of education.[42] The catechists to whom Gregory addresses himself had been trained in dogmatic theology, and he speaks to them as a Christian philosopher. He explains in the preface how their purpose must be to adapt their teaching to suit the needs of each candidate for baptism according to the religious beliefs that he held before conversion. The same approach will not do for Jew, Manichaean, pagan, and Gnostic.[43] Gregory's treatise deals with three basic doctrines—the Trinity, the Incarnation, and the sacraments of baptism and the Eucharist. Apart from the revelation of the author's own dogmatic position, which does not concern us, the work strikingly illustrates the extraordinary mixture of religious beliefs and cult that still existed in the empire *circa* A.D. 385. Thus a heavy obligation rested on the Christian teacher of being adequately equipped for a difficult task—to convince prospective converts of good education that the religious tenets or rites to which they had hitherto given their allegiance were founded in error. In the prologue Gregory lists a number of heresies; in the body of the treatise he censures the Jews and also the pagans.[44] But the only opponents whom he attacks in more than general terms are the Manichaeans. The reason for this is not far to seek. To the orthodox Christian Mani and his followers were peculiarly obnoxious. They rejected the Old Testament, and they taught a dualism which in effect denied the infinite goodness of God, because it opposed to the Creator a Power of Evil in constant conflict with Him. Furthermore, at the time when Gregory was writing, this heresy was very prevalent, not only in the eastern provinces but in the West, where for a few years it ensnared even Augustine.

In the Latin-speaking West, apart from Augustine's treatise, the material illustrating catechetical instruction is less abundant and less detailed than the material in the Greek Fathers. Several tracts by Tertullian, all of them dating from his pre-Montanist period, were composed with the needs of catechumens at least partly in mind. Each is devoted to a single topic; together they exemplify the two main duties of the catechist, to warn and to instruct. Thus in one tract he denounces the public shows and theaters, in another, intended for female converts, he condemns luxury in dress and love of jewelry and counsels simplicity in attire on all occasions. Three other works explain the meaning and proper function of prayer, penance, and baptism. The *De mysteriis* by Ambrose is a counterpart, though seemingly independent of them, to the five "mystagogic" addresses by John of Jerusalem; for it was intended for the newly baptized and reveals the inner meaning of the sacraments of baptism and the Eucharist. The work entitled *De Abraham* is made up of two distinct treatises. The first is addressed to catechumens and represents Abraham as the ideal man of God and hence a pattern to emulate; the second, intended for the baptized, applies the method of categorical interpretation to the patriarch's life and work. All these writings by Tertullian and Ambrose have one common feature: in their published form, at least, they can only have been suitable for educated members of the congregation; for, although Tertullian alludes in one place to those who are content simply to believe, all his tracts and Ambrose's also would have proved obscure, if not incomprehensible, to converts with little or no schooling.[45] Thus they contrast strongly with a short sermon in which Augustine elucidates the Lord's prayer in simple language to catechumens and with the remains of six addresses by Niceta, which have a special interest of their own.[46] Bishop of the remote see of Remesiana, now Ak Palanka, a little east of Nish in Jugoslavia, Niceta was pastor of a flock composed predominantly of only half-romanized peasants. His sermons are therefore couched in easy, straightforward Latin suitable for these "rustic souls," even when he is touching on abstruse points of dogma. But he had to contend with other difficulties than lack of education—difficulties which to some extent confronted any catechist, but which were greatly enhanced in his frontier see. The vicinity of Goths who were heretics increased the danger of false teaching, and it is no accident that Niceta, who enumerates half a dozen heresies, pays special attention to Arianism. He also utters emphatic warnings against "cults, idols, divination, and augury," because, as we have already seen, such heathen practices were particularly rife and tenacious in country districts. His fourth address is unhappily lost, but its title, *Against Casting Horoscopes at Birth* (*Adversus genethliologiam*), coupled with the fact that he devoted a whole sermon to this topic, proves how grave in his eyes was the peril threatening his congregation from astrology and other ways of forecasting the future. For the rest, his purpose, like that of other catechists, was to make intelligible to simple folk the basic tenets of orthodox Christianity, and especially the Creed, which he expounded phrase by phrase.[47] If, as is most likely, he was the author of the *Te Deum,* the noblest of all Christian hymns, then he was also a poet of no mean order. Lastly, if one may judge Niceta's personality from what little remains of his writings, one will readily agree with Zeiller who calls him "one of those doctors of the Church who are in harmony with the inner conviction of Christian people, one for whom Christianity is not a system but above all a way of life." [48]

To sum up: An attempt has been made, by assembling evidence from both Eastern and Western sources, to illustrate in some detail the life of the Christian communities during the later empire in one of its most vital aspects.

There were variations necessitated by local conditions; for what was suitable for the sophisticated townsmen of Antioch might not be adapted to the needs of rough farmers in Dacia, and the problems confronting the catechist in Alexandria, Milan, or even Carthage would differ from those that he would encounter in the rural areas of Gaul or Spain. But in essentials the procedure that had been evolved through the years was uniform and had stood the test of time. If the victory of Christianity over its rivals resulted above all from the admirable organization which the leaders of the Church, in imitation of the secular Roman government in its best days, had slowly but surely perfected, the inner cohesion and solidarity of the Christian communities were achieved by the unremitting care with which the ever-growing body of converts, drawn from all sections of the population, were first scrutinized and then instructed until they were ready for the final act of submission and faith.

Chapter III

THE HIGHER EDUCATION

OF CHRISTIANS

IN THE previous chapters we have passed in review two sharply opposed ways of life, particularly as expressed in terms of educational theory and practice—the training of the pagan in rhetoric and philosophy and the purely religious instruction imparted to Christian converts. It remains to consider the reconciliation of these two extremes in the Christian writers of the third and fourth centuries; to examine the character and extent of the compromise by which a part of the pagan heritage became adapted to the needs of the time and so was transmitted to the medieval world of western Europe.

The official attitude of the Greek and Latin Fathers to the Higher Education of their day was not uniform. While it would be an exaggeration to say of it *quot homines tot sententiae,* various shades of opinion can be observed, and any generalization which implies that all or most of them condemned pagan literature and philosophy without qualification would be completely false. Their objections were obvious. Prose and poetry were inescapably filled with allusions to polytheism, and many of its aspects were far from edifying.[1] Even Plato was not immune from criti-

[For notes to Chapter III, see pages 129–133.]

cism; for, although he advocated censorship over poetry
and the arts, his treatment in the *Phaedrus* and the *Banquet*
of homosexuality was easily open to misconstruction, and
an essential institution in both his ideal and his "second-
best" state was community in wives and children. This, as
Aristotle had already objected, meant the destruction of
family life; and, besides, as Lactantius feelingly remarks,
"how great will be the unhappiness of that city where
women fill the places of men." [2] The dangerous lure of
rhetoric, and especially cleverness in speaking without regard for moral sense, call forth constant warnings, but
high-minded pagans from Aristophanes on had voiced
similar criticisms long before. So one is not surprised to find
the opinion expressed very early that it is better for a Christian to be pious but unlearned, and the Church Orders
recommend that all books of the heathen be avoided:

But avoid all books of the heathen. For what hast thou to do
with strange sayings or laws or lying prophecies which also
turn away from the faith them that are young? What is lacking
to thee in the word of God, that thou shouldst cast thyself upon
these fables of the heathen? If thou wouldst read historical nar-
ratives, thou hast the Book of Kings; but if philosophers and
wise men, thou hast the Prophets, wherein thou shalt find wisdom and understanding more than that of the wise men and
philosophers. And if thou wish for songs, thou hast the Psalms
of David; but if thou wouldst read of the beginning of the world,
thou hast the Genesis of the great Moses; and if laws and com-
mandments, thou hast the glorious Law of the Lord God. All
strange writings therefore which are contrary to these wholly
eschew.[3]

Such sentiments became a commonplace; but, as Christian controversialists knew perfectly well, simple piety was

not enough because one must be able to confute the enemies of Christianity by reasoned argument.[4]

The established system of education was based on the
study of Greek and Latin literature, and it is hard to see
what alternative, at least for the Christian laity, could have
been substituted. The leaders of the Church were for the
most part practical men who accepted what they could not
change but warned against its dangers in varying degrees.
So the Christian small boy in the fourth century was, like
his gentile fellows, copying out the names of the pagan
gods and learning to read from the same old authors.[5] Tertullian is typical of those who, after conversion, were most
hostile to the liberal arts to which they owed the forma-
tion and discipline of their own minds. After inveighing
against the dramatic shows, especially the indecent Atel-
lane farces, he adds the comment that, if comedies and
tragedies dealt with licentious and bloody passions and
crimes, they should not even be read. *"Quod in facto reici-
tur, etiam in dicto non est recipiendum."* [6] Yet, even in the
austerest period of his life when he had turned to Mon-
tanism, he grudgingly allowed the need of some schooling.
It was needful for the business of daily life and even for
learning the truths of Christianity; and once he even admits that there might be some good in pagan philosophy
and that ignorance can be a greater danger than knowledge.[7] Unqualified condemnation, without even the con-
cessions made by Tertullian, are not wanting. A cynic
might, however, find significance in the fact that an Epiphanius or a Lucifer of Calaris, whose opinions are most
violent, were both, stylistically considered, very indifferent writers, and as thinkers not even in the second rank.[8]
What became the normal and, given the changing condi-

tions of the times, the reasonable approach to the problem amounted to an acceptance of the pagan educational system, coupled with the warning that it was to be merely a means to an end and should not be unduly prolonged. This is the position of Basil the Great in his short address to young men on reading the classics. Although pagan literature is inferior to the Scriptures, it is not without value. Some of its poets and prose-writers are worthy of study, namely, those who teach good principles of conduct or who illustrate what they are saying with examples of good men in the past. Indeed, in these authors many instances are recorded of pagans whose patience or other virtues conformed to the precepts of the Gospels; and some of their philosophers have rightly taught that the human soul is far more precious than the body. Thus the young Christian can derive profit from this non-Christian source, provided that he is ever on his guard against what is morally base.[9] The argument was, of course, not new. Two centuries before, Justin Martyr had allowed some merit to the noblest of the pagan thinkers—Heraclitus, Musonius Rufus, and the Platonic Socrates who, "by casting out Homer and the other poets from the commonwealth, taught men to reject evil demons and demons who did what the poets describe." [10] Basil's address, which has often been praised, is really a very slight performance. It omits to point out that pagan culture alone at that date could train the mind and inculcate breadth of view and depth of perception. One hopes that the more discerning of his young hearers derived inspiration rather from the master himself, a pattern of the best Christian pastor who was also steeped in the wisdom of the pagans.

John Chrysostom also conceded the value of the pagan

schools, although his adverse comments outnumber those that are more favorable.[11] Nevertheless, his main point, in which he is merely repeating with a Christian slant what the greatest of the pagan educators, from Plato and Isocrates to Quintilian, had stated emphatically long before, is that the moral purpose of education is more important than anything else. So he can, like Justin or Basil, quote historical examples from the pagan world that are worthy of emulation—Diogenes, Aristides, and Archelaus, the teacher of Socrates. In one of his earliest works he exclaims:

Well then! Some one says, "Shall we raze the schools to the ground?" That is not what I am saying, but that we must not destroy utterly the dwelling place of virtue or bury the living soul. If the soul is prudent, lack of speaking will not result in any loss; but if it is destroyed, the harm done is most serious, even though the tongue happens to be sharp and polished, and the greater the power of speaking, the greater the harm done. . . . The study of eloquence requires good morals, but good morals do not require eloquence.

Near the end of his life, in one of his homilies on Acts, Chrysostom's line of argument, though differently expressed, is still the same.[12] The greatest orator of his age, whose Greek is of classical purity, he exemplifies within himself an all but perfect fusion of old and new. His use of the word *philosophia* is highly instructive both because it illustrates his skill in using a word with various shades of meaning according to the context, and because he is perhaps the earliest Christian author to employ *philosophia* with a purely Christian connotation. Usually when he does so he means the Christian way of life, as when, in one of the latest of his letters, he alludes to a young student of theology entrusted to his care as "practicing the true philosophy." [13] Philosophy consists in disregard of worldly things, in love of mankind, and giving alms. It is the knowledge of things human and divine. It seeks for one thing only, to keep the soul unharmed and safe from all that could hurt it. Pagan philosophers are frequently derided. They are described as bearded, wearing long cloaks, leaning on long staves, and generally offensive, and their philosophy is not worth "three obols" or, as we should say, "two cents." [14] This is the typical satire on the Cynics familiar from Juvenal, Lucian, and others; and, using the inevitable pun, Chrysostom calls them outcasts whose only thought is for their bellies and who are lower than the dogs crouching under the dining table.[15] In his eleventh homily on the Antioch statues there is a sustained passage in which he contrasts the pagan with the Christian interpretation of man and the universe; and in yet another sermon he stresses the transitory nature of human existence and exclaims:

Read, if thou wilt, our writings and those of the pagans, if thou dost despise ours from despair. If thou dost admire the works of the philosophers, proceed even in these. They will teach thee by their tales of ancient disasters, and so will their poets and rhetors and sophists and all their historians. On all sides, if thou wishest, thou wilt find the proofs.[16]

In Basil and even more in Chrysostom one can discern a certain reluctance to give full approval to pagan education. But there were other Greek Fathers who, though not Origenists, had been affected to a marked degree by Origen; in particular they had fallen under the spell of his pedagogy, and this led them to exercise a wide tolerance. Eusebius of Caesarea and Gregory of Nyssa show this by the general character of their writings. Gregory of Nazianzus has put it explicitly into words:

I take it as admitted by men of sense, that the first of our advantages is education; and not only this our more noble form of it, which disregards rhetorical ornaments and glory, and holds to salvation and beauty in the objects of our contemplation; but even that pagan culture which many Christians spit upon, as treacherous and dangerous, and keeping us afar from God. For as we ought not to neglect the heavens, and earth, and air, and all such things, because some have wrongly seized upon them, and honour God's works instead of God: but to reap what advantage we can from them for our life and enjoyment, while we avoid their dangers; not raising creation, as foolish men do, in revolt against the Creator, but from the works of nature apprehending the Worker (Romans 1, 20 and 25), and, as the divine apostle says (II Corinthians 10, 5), bringing into captivity every thought to Christ: and again, as we know that neither fire, nor food, nor iron, nor any other of the elements, is of itself most useful or most harmful, except according to the will of those who use it; and as we have compounded healthful drugs from certain of the reptiles; so from secular literature we have received principles of inquiry and speculation, while we have rejected their idolatry, terror, and pit of destruction. Nay, even those have aided us in our religion, by our perception of the contrast between what is worse and what is better, and by gaining strength for our doctrine from the weakness of theirs. We must not then dishonour education, because some men are pleased to do so, but rather suppose such men to be boorish and uneducated, desiring all men to be as they themselves are, in order to hide what is appropriate to them among the common mass and escape the detection of their want of culture.[17]

We shall see how closely this comprehensive plan of general culture within a Christian framework corresponds to the teaching of Clement and of Origen in Alexandria and Caesarea.

If the sources for the earlier phase of the catechumenate are scanty, they are even less informative about the training of the clergy and the higher education of Christian converts. At the same time reasoned defenses of the Christian position had begun already in the age of Hadrian. Their authors were men who had been brought up as pagans and on their conversion had studied the Scriptures, bringing to their task minds well trained in logical exposition. The earliest of these Apologies, by Quadratus, is lost, but his successors in this branch of literature, Aristides, Justin Martyr, and Athenagoras, can still be judged by their writings.[18] Their purpose was to justify the Christian way of life by demonstrating the purity of its ethical code and to overcome the widespread prejudice felt against the new sect by refuting the various charges leveled against it by pagan and Jewish contemporaries. The assumption that Justin while in Rome was engaged in teaching rests on slight evidence; even less well attested is the statement in a late author that Athenagoras was active as a catechist in Alexandria, since it cannot be reconciled with the only reliable account, that by Eusebius, which we possess of Christian studies in the great center of Graeco-Roman learning.[19] But even Eusebius' information is tantalizingly sparse, so that doubts have been expressed whether there ever was a regularly organized school of higher Christian education in the Egyptian capital.[20] There is, however, no reason to question the reliability of the Church historian who states that a "school of the sacred Writings" was established in Alexandria and that its first teacher was

Pantaenus. This institution certainly continued down to Eusebius' own time and probably to near the end of the fourth century. The successor of Pantaenus was Clement, and he in turn was succeeded by his pupil, Origen. The genius of Origen as a teacher brought him so many pupils that he associated his disciple, Heraclas, with himself in the work of instruction. Later, on Origen's departure from Alexandria, Heraclas took his place. Eusebius names several others who directed the catechetical school, notably Dionysius, but unhappily he does not give a complete list of teachers down to 312, the year in which the first recension of his *Ecclesiastical History* was probably completed. That the institution continued during the fourth century can be deduced from Rufinus whose testimony on the subject there is no reason to question or discard. After describing the astonishing erudition, in spite of his blindness, of Didymus, he calls him teacher of the Church school.[21] Eusebius has nothing to say about organization, though he implies that Origen instructed his pupils in his own house. If, however, we accept the essential point of his account, namely, that during approximately a century and a quarter (180–312) a succession of instructors directed a course of Christian studies, then we are justified in assuming some measure of organization and some continuity of method. The fact that Origen surpassed all others in learning and genius is nothing to the point; whether the teachers received payment for their pupils, as pagan rhetoricians did, or whether the Christian community at any time maintained the school which shed luster on the Alexandrian community and exerted a wide influence beyond, in Asia Minor, Syria, and Palestine, is not known. That the instruction was given in private homes, not in some public place, is again not surprising; for this was a common practice of pagan teachers of rhetoric or philosophy, unless they were fortunate enough to hold an imperial or municipal chair in their subject.

Before his conversion Pantaenus had been a Stoic and Clement bears witness to the inspiring quality of his teaching. Clement himself refers repeatedly in his works to the valuable function of Greek philosophy as a preparation for the reception of the Christian revelation. He compares its influence on the Greeks to the educative power exercised on the Jews by their Law. Greek philosophy was indeed a divine gift granted to them so that they might understand the truth of the Gospel. In his *Paedagogus* or *Educator* Clement laid down the way of life which, in his opinion, the Christian must follow. In judging this work, and in fact all his writings, one must remember that he wrote at a time when the Christians were still a persecuted sect. He himself was forced to leave Alexandria at the time of the persecutions under Septimius Severus (*circa* A.D. 203), to spend the last twelve years or so of his life in Asia Minor. Furthermore, the Church, in spite of many trials, had become a highly organized institution. Its members were to be found in most, if not yet all, the provinces of the empire, and many of the most recent converts were highly educated pagans. The *Paedagogus*, from Whom Clement's treatise derives its name, is Christ, or rather the *Logos*, the Word made flesh (John 1:14); the relationship between Him and the new convert is as that of a father to his child. The emphasis in the first book of the treatise is on faith (*Pistis*). In Clement's later work, the *Stromata*, he sets out at length the steps by which the Christian should advance to knowledge or understanding (*Gnosis*). *Gnosis* is not in opposition to *Pistis;* rather it consists in a fuller comprehension of what is already implicit in faith. Baptism to Clement is illumination, and *Gnosis* is bestowed by baptism and by God's Grace which is received with that sacrament.[22] Clement's purpose as a teacher and author was, broadly speaking, twofold: to controvert the Gnostics of his day whose preoccupation with philosophy and sometimes with religious ideas of paganism had led them into heterodoxy or heresy; and, at the same time, to convince those of his Christian contemporaries who rejected everything in pagan thought as dangerous to belief, that it was possible for an orthodox Christian to acquire a knowledge of dialectic and the best philosophical thought —Stoicism and Platonism as understood in his day—and also a proper understanding of the physical universe. So far from harming the faith of a Christian, this knowledge would help to deepen his understanding of the truth of Christianity. In expounding the Old Testament and the New, Clement, like Origen after him, made extensive use of allegorical interpretation, in itself a heritage from Jewish scholarship and in particular from Philo of Alexandria.

The second and third Books of the *Paedagogus* are a practical guide to the Christian way of life on earth. Clement lays down directions for behavior at all times, by day and night, in the house and abroad. Much that he says necessarily consists of warnings against all those aspects of contemporary society which were incompatible with the proper conduct of a Christian—luxury in dress or in household goods, drunkenness, incontinence, gambling, the theater and shows. On the positive side em-

phasis is laid on the moral qualities that must distinguish
a Christian, in essence an exposition of the Ten Command-
ments together with instructions on churchgoing and
prayer. His discussion of Christian marriage is marked by
great frankness, but the subject is treated with a sympa-
thetic understanding rare in the Patristic authors. It is a
fair assumption, though it cannot be proved, that
Clement's extant writings are an elaboration of the
material which he had presented in simpler form to his
pupils in the catechetical school.[23] It does not, moreover,
seem to have been sufficiently observed that this hypothesis
is confirmed by other evidence than Clement's own works.
The wide variety of topics discussed and the attempt
to harmonize the best of pagan thought with the teaching of the Bible have their counterpart in the curriculum
laid down by Origen, which is described with some full-
ness by one of his pupils.

Gregory Thaumaturgus, though intended for a career
in the imperial service, followed his own inclination when
opportunity offered. So, instead of attending the law
school at Berytus, he became a pupil of Origen's in
Caesarea; and as Origen is not likely to have changed
either his aims or his methods in any important respect
when he moved from Egypt to Palestine, Gregory's evidence is valid for the whole of Origen's career as a teacher.
The curriculum had as its essential purpose the utiliza-
tion of the best that the liberal arts could offer, to form a
solid foundation for the final stages of instruction. Thus
the training began with teaching the accurate use of language, not so that the pupil would shine as a speaker or
writer, but so that he would be able to express his ideas
as accurately as possible. From this the students passed

to the sciences, elementary biology and physiology, geometry, and astronomy. Next came a study of ethics and particularly the meaning and application of the cardinal virtues. Lastly, the student was ready to proceed to the study and interpretation of the Scriptures. Gregory relates the care with which his teacher used the dialectic method, questioning and arguing with his disciples and setting them problems for solution. Furthermore, he urged them to read all kinds of writings with the exception of those "composed by atheists who . . . denied the existence of God or of Providence." And he continues:

No subject was forbidden us, nothing hidden or inaccessible. We were allowed to become acquainted with every doctrine, barbarian or Greek, with things spiritual and secular, divine and human, traversing with all confidence (cf. Acts 28, 31) and investigating the whole circuit of knowledge, and satisfying ourselves with the full enjoyment of all pleasures of the soul.[24]

The similarity of this enlightened program of study to that which can be reconstructed from the treatises of Clement of Alexandria is obvious. And there is a further point of likeness: Clement also had read, and doubtless encouraged his pupils to read, literature and philosophy over a wide field. But, just as Origen had made an exception of atheistical writings, so Clement had excluded Epicurus and his followers from serious consideration.[25]

Before passing to the great Latin Fathers of the fourth century, we must refer once more to the last of the pagan philosophies. The impact of Neoplatonism on Christianity was profound. Among the earlier works of Porphyry, the disciple and successor of Plotinus, was an elaborate polemic against the new religion, which called forth rebuttals from the Christian side. The destruction of all copies of this treatise was ordered by Constantine, an action which has been termed "the first instance of the secular arm proceeding against a work of the mind (*une oeuvre de l'esprit*) on the ground of heterodoxy." [26] However that may be, the student of comparative religion may be disposed to agree with Lessing that he would willingly exchange an extant Patristic work for a complete text of Porphyry's lost book.[27] Porphyry's other writings continued to be more frequent targets for attack by Christians than those of any other Neoplatonist. And yet the thinking of the Fathers was deeply affected by the philosophical school which openly they condemned. Gregory of Nyssa in the East and Augustine in the West are the most familiar instances. But often the Christian authors seek to disguise the fact, and it is only through modern research that the extent of their indebtedness is being more fully revealed. Thus, for example, it has been shown recently that Basil the Great and Ambrose not merely had a general acquaintance with Neoplatonism as understood in their day, but had read the *Enneads* of Plotinus himself.[28] But it was not in this imperfect and diluted form alone that Neoplatonic ideas were transmitted to western Europe. More direct was the influence exerted by the works of the writer known to scholars as the pseudo-Dionysius. Composed at the beginning of the sixth century, they profess to be from the hand of Dionysius the Areopagite, the disciple of St. Paul (Acts 17:34). In content they are a kind of Christianized Neoplatonism, their author being very heavily indebted to the last of the great Neoplatonists, Proclus of Athens. These writings are in truth one of the most successful literary frauds of all time. Because the authorship of Dionysius was not seriously called in question, they were received with the respect or even veneration due to works of the sub-Apostolic age. They first became known in the West soon after the beginning of the ninth century in a Latin rendering by Abbot Hilduin.[29] Some fifty years after, they received a wider currency because they were again translated by John the Scot, and John's own works were also profoundly affected by the older writer. Other, more accurate, versions appeared later in the Middle Ages, and the authorship and authenticity of Dionysius were not challenged until 1457. A further reason for the high regard in which these treatises were held in medieval Europe and in some quarters, despite the demonstration of Laurentius Valla that they were pseudepigraphical, until very recent times, was the grotesque but generally accepted identification of Dionysius with St. Denys, the patron saint of France.

We turn finally to the three great Latin Fathers of the fourth century. The eldest of the three, Ambrose, was the son of a government official and himself followed a career in the imperial service until his reluctant consecration, probably at the end of 375, as bishop of Milan. His baptism, as so often in that age, had been postponed and did not take place until a week before he assumed his clerical office. That such a man would have enjoyed all the advantages of higher education in his day could be safely assumed, even if we had not his own writings to prove it. One of these is directly relevant to the subject of this chapter. The treatise, *De officiis ministrorum,* is modeled on the *De officiis* of Cicero, which was itself largely an adaptation from Panaetius. Ambrose, therefore, in composing the first systematic manual of Christian ethics, took a pagan work and recast it, so that it would be suitable for the young clerics for whom it was written. He followed Cicero in the general arrangement, though not slavishly, and at times quotes him verbally, at times paraphrases him. But he also made substantial additions of his own, and for Cicero's examples drawn from Greek and Roman history and literature he substituted others taken from the Bible and particularly from the Old Testament. The final result was a book indubitably Christian in thought, but one in which the best elements of Stoic teaching, which did not conflict with Christian doctrine, also found a place. The method followed illustrates an important principle adopted also, as we shall see, by Augustine, that of rewriting a Ciceronian treatise of established authority. Not undeservedly Ambrose's book was widely read throughout the medieval period; it was also for centuries one of the chief sources from which the Middle Ages derived their knowledge of Stoic ethics.

The writings of Origen, in spite of his heterodoxy, deeply influenced later generations of Christian scholars not only in the East but also in the West, and of this there is no clearer example than Jerome. His great reputation as a *vir trilinguis*, one familiar with Greek and Hebrew in addition to his native Latin, was deserved but must be judged in the light of the age in which he lived. In the western provinces of the empire the knowledge of Greek had declined steadily ever since the third century, and by the time of Jerome's birth in 347 it seems to have been confined to a small minority. A generation later some of those who sang Greek liturgical chants that were still in use at Rome could not understand the words that they were singing.[30] Jerome may have begun to learn Greek in Rome; but he acquired a more thorough knowledge of the language subsequently during his first extended visit to the East. His essential purpose was to deepen his theological studies; hence, while he read intensively in Origen and supplemented this by portions of Clement and of Greek theologians of more recent date, he had only a limited acquaintance with the poets and prose writers of pagan Greece.[31] Then he set himself the further task of mastering the original language in which the Old Testament was composed and enlisted the help of some of the best Jewish teachers of the time in Syria and Palestine.[32] To understand how very unusual this effort to learn Hebrew then was, one must remember that the use of the Septuagint and other Greek versions of the Old Testament was universal, and that even men like John Chrysostom and Theodore of Mopsuestia, who lived and worked in the midst of a population that was largely Semitic, were ignorant of Hebrew.[33] Latin literature and thought, however, had formed the substance of Jerome's thought in Dalmatia and later in Rome, where Donatus had been one of his teachers, and his schooling had consisted of the usual program with *grammaticus* and *rhetor*, supplemented by some instruction in philosophy. Numerous quotations and reminiscences from Virgil, Horace, Persius, Cicero, and Quintilian, with an occasional echo of Plautus, Terence, Lucretius, and Juvenal, are scattered through his works from first to last.[34] Thus his mind was richly stocked with historical examples drawn from classical antiquity. When, for instance, he alludes to attacks on himself and his writings, he refers by way of comparison to the detractors of Terence, Cicero, and Virgil. Each profession should imitate the best exponents of it. After illustrating this principle by reference to the greatest of the pagan generals, philosophers, historians, and orators, he demands that, similarly, the Christian clergy should take as their guides the best models, that is the Apostles and their companions.[35] "Bodily excellences change with age and, while wisdom alone increases, the others decay," he remarks on another occasion, and, again by way of example names certain philosophers and poets of yore.[36] He abhors rhetoric for rhetoric's sake and, though conceding some value to philosophy, attacks its tenets on specific questions where they conflict with Christian doctrine. Writing to Ctesiphon in 414, he rejects the theories of philosophers on the passions and quotes Tertullian's dictum about the philosophers being "the patriarchs of the heretics"; but then the main purpose of this letter is to controvert the views of Pelagius.[37] In particular, like other Christian writers, he notes with alarm the use made by heresiarchs of the Aristotelian dialectic. "Unskilled heretics," he says, "are hard to find; for all heretics are teachers trained in secular knowledge. Theirs not the net of the Apostolic fisherman, but the little chains of dialectic." [38]

It would be easy to misinterpret Jerome's opinion of contemporary higher education. He complains constantly of attacks leveled at him either as a translator or commentator.[39] The result on a high-strung, indeed somewhat "touchy," nature was that the controversialist in him is rarely dormant. For this reason two letters addressed in 395 to Paulinus of Nola are of exceptional value.[40] Both epistles were, so far as anything from Jerome's pen ever could be, written *sine ira et studio;* for, if he expresses

himself with some warmth, it is not controversy but his
passion for Biblical study and his anxiety about the
theological training of Paulinus, recently turned monk,
that call it forth. In the well-known letter to the Roman
rhetorician, Magnus (*Epist.* 70), though it supplements
our knowledge, Jerome is on the defensive, as he suspects
that his correspondent had allowed himself to become the
mouthpiece of Rufinus, by that time Jerome's bitter enemy.
In the earlier letter to Paulinus he urges him to seek not
a great city like Jerusalem, but solitude in which to
pursue his studies, and he compliments him on his pane-
gyric addressed to Theodosius:

You have a great intellect and an inexhaustible store of language, your diction is fluent and pure, your fluency and purity
are mingled with wisdom. Your head is clear and all your
senses are keen. Were you to add to this wisdom and eloquence
a careful study and knowledge of Scripture, I should soon see
you holding our citadel against all comers; you would go up
with Joab upon the roofs of Zion (I Chronicles 11, 5–6) and
sing upon the housetops what you had learned in the secret
chambers (cf. Luke 12, 3).[41]

The core of the second letter is a brief guide to the
study of Scripture. Jerome begins by describing the zeal
for learning which many famous pagans had displayed
and then passes on to St. Paul and to the Apostles Peter
and John, whose wisdom was inspired by God. Every-
one imagines that he can interpret the Bible, but the results are disastrous. Biblical exegesis, on the contrary,
must be learned like any other branch of human knowledge, and this process involves three things—teaching,
method, and practice or proficiency. He uses the Greek
terms for these words, which closely recall the threefold

division first enunciated by the early sophists; [42] but he omits the natural disposition of the student and considers teaching under two aspects. As for the untutored interpreters, though their words may charm the ear, they misrepresent what they have read and distort the meaning to suit their own views. Jerome then rapidly passes the books of the Old and New Testaments in review and indicates some of the lessons that they can teach. He censures mere verbal dexterity and ingenuity in argument, but it is abundantly clear all through both letters to Paulinus that he demands a sound education along established lines—in short, one similar to his own—from those who are to instruct other Christians. Indeed he goes even beyond this, when he observes: "A saintly lack of education benefits only a man himself, and what he achieves by the excellence of his life in building up the Church of Christ is counterbalanced by the harm that he does it, if he does not oppose those who speak against it." [43] Against this evidence the many passages where he is critical of particular aspects of pagan literature or thought weigh lightly in the balance. One may regret that he never sat down to compose a manual of Christian hermeneutics, but what he failed to undertake was accomplished by his great contemporary in North Africa.

Augustine's *De doctrina Christiana* reproduces two phases of his thought on education; for, although two-thirds of it were written down in 397, the remainder was not finished until 426. At that date he enlarged the third book by adding a detailed discussion of Tyconius' seven rules for interpreting the Bible and composed Book 4. He himself explains that three books of the treatise as revised and augmented were intended to aid the under-

standing of the sacred text, and the fourth to teach the
right method of expressing and transmitting to others what
has been understood.[44] The work is, in short, a manual
of hermeneutics and homiletics. Its author begins by discussing the nature of God and the operation of the Divine
Wisdom insofar as comprehensible to man. The way to
God is through Christ, and in essence the complete teaching of the Scriptures is comprised in the injunctions to
love God and to love one's neighbor. Even though our
interpretation of the Bible be faulty, it does not lie or de-
ceive, if only it serves the end of inducing this love. In
considering words and their proper use, Augustine touches
on the diversity of languages and on certain obscurities
in the sacred text. The use of the canonical books of the
Old and New Testaments which he enumerates and some
observations on their translations lead to a long section
on preliminary studies that are useful and indeed necessary for the Biblical expositor and preacher. Pagan writings can be of value, provided they are rightly used and
their dangers avoided. Augustine surveys the whole pagan system of education as comprised in the seven liberal
arts. The inherent perils are illustrated particularly with
reference to the sciences, because they, as taught by the
gentiles, may contain or lead to superstition and worse.
He has in mind magic and especially astrology which
results from a misuse of astronomical science, and his
strictures are yet another proof of the extraordinary hold
which the pseudo-science had on both the educated and
uneducated classes of his day.[45] He comes next to the
interpretation of the Scriptures and shows the various ways
in which ambiguity can arise in a given passage and how
the difficulty can often be resolved by reference to other

passages. He himself was, like the Alexandrian theologians and in opposition to the Antiochene school of divines, a doughty champion of the allegorical method. So in *De doctrina Christiana*, taking as his text the words of the Apostle (II Corinthians 3:6), "The letter killeth, but the spirit giveth life," he warns against undue adherence to the literal sense; he also observes that a particular word or phrase may mean different things in different contexts. The later addition to the third book summarizes at considerable length the teaching of Tyconius. Caution must be used when studying this author, partly because he writes as a Donatist and therefore a heretic, partly because, as any human being must, he made some mistakes. But one may agree with Tyconius' modern editor that Augustine "treats Tyconius as an authority to be explained rather than as a theorist to be criticised." [46]

When Augustine composed Book 4 he adopted a procedure analogous to that followed by Ambrose, who, as we have seen, adapted Cicero's dialogue on moral duties to Christian ends. Similarly Augustine turned to Cicero's rhetorical works, and especially to the *Orator,* for the broad framework of his treatise and the general theory of oratorical composition. Moreover, just as Ambrose had substituted Biblical for pagan examples to illustrate various moral qualities or their opposites, so Augustine gives examples of the three types of oratory drawn from the writings of St. Paul, Cyprian, and Ambrose. But, unlike Ambrose, who often reproduces phrases and sentences from Cicero word for word, Augustine writes throughout in his own language and very rarely makes a direct quotation from his pagan sources. Nevertheless, his debt to Cicero is not superficial; for the parallelism in thought between the classical theory of oratory and Augustine's theory of Christian preaching can be traced right through the book.[47]

Augustine's book gave his contemporaries a clear and self-contained guide for the whole education of a Christian teacher. But its immense popularity in later centuries can easily mislead one into overrating its quality.[48] Considered on its own merits it is neither profound nor greatly original. The section on the liberal arts, moreover, and the standard of attainment in them that he demands are so elementary that they throw a vivid light on the startling decline in the intellectual life of the Roman empire that had come about in the course of one hundred and fifty years. To say this is not to detract from Augustine, but simply to put on record that, greatly as he stood above his contemporaries as a theologian and Christian philosopher, he was still a child of his age and bound by the limitations of that age. It must not be forgotten, however, that for some three centuries after his death the classical heritage survived in western Europe precariously and to a great degree indirectly through works like the two treatises of Ambrose and Augustine. Although manuscripts of the Latin classics were preserved, they remained for the most part forgotten and unread, until the remarkable revival of interest in pagan Latin literature which got under way in the time of Charlemagne and grew rapidly under his immediate successors. The official attitude of churchmen and authors continued variable; for it is a complete misconception to assert that, by and large, they were enemies of the classics. At all times there were some intransigent spirits. We find them in the ninth century and again at intervals throughout the Middle

Ages. The controversy about the use of pagan authors was resurrected in the sixteenth century and cropped up from time to time right down to the nineteenth. As late as 1851, at the height of the disputes in France between the Gallicans and Ultramontanes, the Abbé Gaume published a volume bearing the sensational title, *Le Ver rongeur des sociétés modernes.* Its subtitle, *Le Paganisme dans l'éducation,* which was adopted by itself for the English translation issued in 1852, indicates the contents of the book. It was an impassioned plea that the classics be banned, if not from all secondary schools, at least from schools and seminaries which trained young men for the priesthood. Although the book caused a considerable stir when it was published, it failed in its purpose; for in 1853 Pius IX in an encyclical approved the continued use of the classics, though with the necessary precautions and along with Patristic literature.

In conclusion, the continuity in respect to literature and scholarship between antiquity and the Middle Ages was never broken, and it was the Latin Fathers of the fourth century, and after them Cassiodorus and Isidore, whose works form a bridge from one epoch to the other. The later Roman imperial age, which has formed the subject of these lectures, was a period of steady decline. The Carolingian age was one of rediscovery, traditionalism, and also stabilization. Its theologians, with the solitary exception of John the Scot, ventured on no new paths of intellectual adventure. They studied the writers of the Patristic age and in their own works reproduced the views of the Fathers directly, or else adapted and simplified them for the benefit of their students and readers. The rediscovery—for it was no less than that—of

Latin poets and prose writers of pagan Rome bore fruit in two ways. They became models for imitation, as we can see in the elegiac verse of a Theodulfus or an Alcuin, or the alcaic and sapphic stanzas composed with considerable skill by Sedulius of Liége. In prose the most obvious example of the same trend is Einhard's biography of Charlemagne, much of which is closely modeled on Suetonius' *Lives of the Caesars.* The second, and historically more momentous, effect of the rediscovery was an intense and widespread activity in the writing schools of cathedrals and monasteries. If it had not been for the devoted efforts of copyists and librarians during the eighth and ninth centuries, the surviving authors of Latin antiquity would be far fewer than they are, and the state of our extant texts would be decidedly worse than it is. The Carolingian age, which was the heir of classical antiquity, marks the culmination of the first stage in the long intellectual history of medieval and modern Europe.

APPENDIX

Introduction

JOHN CHRYSOSTOM'S *Address on Vainglory and the Right Way for Parents to Bring Up Their Children* has survived in two manuscripts, *Parisinus graecus* 764, foll. 314v–343v, and Lesbos 42, foll. 92v–118r, but the Lesbos codex has never been collated.[1] Both manuscripts were copied late in the tenth or early in the eleventh century. The *editio princeps*, based on the sole testimony of the *Parisinus*, appeared in Paris in 1656. It was the work of the Dominican scholar, François Combefis, who added a Latin translation. The tract was, however, not included in collected editions of Chrysostom's works because its authenticity was questioned, and so it was not until 1914 that a new edition of the Greek text was brought out by Franz Schulte.[2] He also used only the codex in Paris, but he restored a number of manuscript readings which Combefis had unnecessarily emended. In spite of this long interval between the two editions of the original text, the address did not remain in complete obscurity, partly because the Latin translation by Combefis was reprinted on several occasions, partly because an English version of the second and

[For notes to the Introduction, see page 134.]

longer portion was published anonymously in 1659 by the diarist, John Evelyn. Copies of the two printings made in that year are now exceedingly rare collectors' items; but this translation, together with some other short essays by Evelyn, was reissued in 1825 by William Upcott.[3] A German version by S. Haidacher appeared in 1907. He added a valuable introduction and a selection of extracts from various homilies by Chrysostom in which education and kindred topics were discussed.[4] One of Haidacher's greatest services was to prove conclusively that the treatise was genuine and that the doubts of the Benedictine editors and others had been unjustified. His book is also valuable because his deep familiarity with Chrysostom's writings enabled him to quote many parallels from the homilies. The translation itself, though elegant and readable, is sometimes so free that it becomes a mere paraphrase. Evelyn's version is incomplete because he omitted the opening section on vainglory. This is understandable, as he made the translation under the influence of his own domestic sorrow. It may be admitted that the transition in the address from one part to the other is abrupt; but sudden digressions from his main theme are exceedingly characteristic of Chrysostom's oratorical manner. His genius as a speaker was such, his ideas and imagery were so copious that, as soon as a new thought struck him, he had to give it instant expression. Such "asides" are natural and unforced, and he returns easily to his main theme. When we remember, therefore, that he regarded vainglory as at the root of the moral and social evils which his system of education was meant to remedy, we can see that the connection in thought is very close, even though the verbal transition is sudden. Evelyn's version is distinguished by the dignity and literary skill that one would expect from its author; but it is far from accurate. He sometimes slides over difficult passages—one may suspect that in such cases he paid more attention to Combefis' Latin translation than to the Greek original—sometimes he makes palpable errors. An amusing example of this occurs in paragraph 53.

The address is composed in the style of a homily; indeed it is conceivable that it was actually delivered before a group of parents. Chrysostom constantly employs the second person, sometimes in the singular when he directs his counsel at the individual parent, sometimes in the plural as though he were addressing a congregation. It has seemed best to retain the distinction in English, even though the use of the second person singular may produce a slightly archaic flavor. But to have done otherwise would have been to obliterate one of the most vivid features in the address. There are many parallels in thought between this work and other writings by Chrysostom. The more significant have been pointed out in the notes. Some of his citations from the Old Testament do not correspond exactly to the Septuagint text, the reason doubtless being that he was quoting from memory. Amazing though his knowledge of the Bible must have been—it has been calculated that there are not less than eighteen thousand quotations from the Old and New Testaments in his works—it is not surprising that he occasionally lapsed from strict verbal accuracy.

There is no reason to assume that he consulted other educational writings; for it is mistaken to postulate his indebtedness to the treatise on the education of boys wrongly ascribed to Plutarch. There are no citations in Chrysostom from the earlier writer, and the fact that they express similar views on certain topics proves nothing. Both depre-

cate corporal punishment, both point out the need of occasional relaxation from work, both stress that the boy
should be trained in courtesy even to slaves, both are
advocates of early marriage on moral grounds. But Quintilian, an author with whom Chrysostom, who knew no
Latin, was certainly not familiar, held similar opinions.
Like Chrysostom, he insists that the father should give
careful thought to the education of his boy from the very
first, and the warmth with which Quintilian condemns
luxury, effeminacy, and the vicious influences in Roman
society would have had Chrysostom's cordial approval.[5]
Not only could two writers thinking about the same subject independently arrive at similar views, but some of
these had certainly become a part of the common stock of
ideas among thinking and educated persons long before
the fourth century. One would not labor what in truth is
obvious, were it not that the vicious misuse of *Quellenfor-
schung* still persists. Toward the end of the tract Chrysostom adopts Plato's threefold division of the soul. There can
have been few features of the Platonic philosophy more
familiar to the educated public than this. The influence of
the philosophical schools is apparent also in vocabulary.
Chrysostom has a fondness for the verb $\dot{\rho}\nu\theta\mu\dot{\iota}\zeta\epsilon\iota\nu$ in the
sense of "to train"; it is a usage already found in Plato,
Xenophon, and the Stoics. More striking is his reference
to the "tension of the soul," for this appears to be in origin
a purely Stoic phrase.[6]

What is the date of the address? The question has been
discussed at length, and some critics have assigned it to
Chrysostom's latest period when he was at Constantinople.
Others, however, regard it as an early work. Thus Haidacher argues strongly that the address was composed at

Antioch, while Schulte, though accepting Haidacher's arguments in the main, is inclined to be skeptical and ends by
leaving the problem undecided. Baur, without discussing
the evidence, assumes that the tract is an early work written
about the same time as the homilies against the enemies of
monasticism. Max von Bonsdorff agrees with Haidacher
that the address dates from the same period as the tenth
and eleventh homilies on Ephesians. But he would assign
these to A.D. 396–397, thus attributing *On Vainglory* to the
very end of Chrysostom's Antiochene period.[7] It is, however, dangerous to build arguments on particular passages
in the work. Those who argue in favor of a Constantino-
politan date rely heavily on the description of the rich man
(paragraph 4), whose prodigality in living and entertaining
the people with games has reduced him to the condition
of a pauper without friends, almost a perfect example of the
classical hybris and nemesis. It has been maintained that
Chrysostom, when he drew this graphic picture, was allud-
ing to the disgrace and downfall of Arcadius' minister, Eutropius, in July, 399. The argument is weak, for there is really
very little similarity between the two cases. Eutropius'
ruin resulted not from his extravagance but from his corrupt administration, coupled with the bitter enmity to him
of Stilicho, Gainas, and the empress Eudoxia.[8] Besides, the
evils of worldly wealth, vainglory, and the pride that comes
before the fall had become a commonplace of Christian
preachers, though few, if any, could approach Chrysostom's
vivid eloquence.[9] Again, although Schulte would brush this
objection aside, the allusion to the bishop (paragraph 83)
would be a reference to Chrysostom himself, if the treatise
had been composed in Constantinople. This is not in character; for, when he wishes to draw attention to himself as the

head of his flock, he does so unequivocally.[10] Haidacher maintains that the address and the tenth and eleventh homilies on Ephesians were composed about the same time because of a supposed resemblance between the opening paragraph of *On Vainglory* and a passage in the tenth homily which describes a conflagration destroying a great house, and another in the eleventh homily that alludes to the great beast lacerating the body of the Church. Certainly the dissensions of which Chrysostom speaks in the homily are those that had racked the Church in Antioch ever since the time of Constantius. But what of Chrysostom's tenure of the see of Constantinople? It too was disturbed constantly by faction and disunion within the Church—the quarrel between Chrysostom and Theophilus of Alexandria, the deposition, by Chrysostom's orders though their validity was challenged, of unworthy prelates in Asia Minor, and the attempts of Severianus of Gabala to outshine Chrysostom in the pulpit.

The truth is that there is no satisfactory criterion for dating the address. It contains many passages to which it is possible to find parallels in thought or even in diction in the vast collection of Chrysostom's homilies. But some of these, even when they can be approximately dated, were composed at Antioch, others in Constantinople. The chronology of his sermons, taken as a whole, is not certain; for not all of von Bonsdorff's conclusions are sound. His arguments to prove that a particular series of New Testament homilies was delivered in Antioch or in Constantinople are valid, but his attempts to assign them to a particular year or years are not always convincing. He is also inclined, as others before him have been, to assume that, because two passages in two different homilies resemble one another in thought or diction, they must belong to the same period of Chrysostom's life. But to argue thus is to ignore the plain fact that, with all his inexhaustible variety of expression, metaphor, and illustrative examples, the preacher recurs again and again and at different periods of his life to the same broad topics. One of these is the education, or rather the moral training, of the young; others are the dangers of riches and vanity and their resultant evils, the immorality of the times as shown in the circus and the theater, and the prevalence of pederasty. Vice in all its forms was ever in the mind of the preacher who, in this capacity, was far more interested in raising the standard of public morals than in doctrinal subtleties. Hannah and the wisdom with which she reared the boy Samuel not only form the subject matter for five special sermons, but are introduced elsewhere, whenever Chrysostom desires to stress the right training of character as the principal aim of Christian education. In paragraph 61 of the address he says: "Let him hear the whole story of Joseph continually." This is another of the *exempla* drawn from the Old Testament which he uses again and again. The necessity of early marriage for Christian youths, to obviate the danger of illicit unions, is still another topic on which he loves to dwell, and coupled with it we often find condemnation of pagan marriage customs with their unseemly frivolities. He considers the question also from the point of view of finding a worthy husband for the bride-to-be. Thus he says: "Look not to money or illustrious lineage or to the importance of his native place. All these are superfluous. Look rather to the piety and goodness of his soul, to true understanding and fear of the Lord, if thou wouldst have thy daughter live happily." [11] In the ninth homily on I Timothy Chrysostom gives some general directions on the bringing up of children, which seem to epitomize what he has stated more fully in the address: "Bring up your children in the nurture and admonition of the Lord (Ephesians 6:4) with much correction. Youth is a wild thing and needs many to be set over it, teachers, tutors, attendants, nurses; for even with so many safeguards it can scarce be kept in check. Like unto some untamed steed, some untamable wild creature, such is youth." [12] The close similarity to opinions expressed in the address *On Vainglory* of the two passages just quoted is obvious; yet one of them was composed in Constantinople, the other in Antioch! The emphasis on the ethical side of education which recurs so often in the homilies is found already in one of the earliest of his works, the treatise against the enemies of the monks. There too we find similarities in thought to our tract: "The boy's soul, if rightly trained, will daily become fairer, like a statue growing under the hands of the artist." The right training of youth is likened to the training of Olympic victors, the example of Hannah and Samuel is introduced, and in the final exhortation the fathers who bring up their sons in the proper way are called "fathers who are builders of temples in which Christ dwells and the guardians of heavenly athletes." [13]

It would be possible to draw up an extended list of quotations from the sermons, in each of which some likeness in thought occurs to the sentiments found in the address *On Vainglory*. But it must suffice to draw attention to three parallels which are more than superficially close. Near the beginning of the address (paragraph 3) there is an allusion to Dead Sea fruit or "Apples of Sodom." This phenomenon is explained more fully in the eighth homily on I Thessalonians. The homilies on this Pauline epistle were certainly composed in Constantinople; so that, if one were to assume, on the strength of this example, that the sermon and the address were composed about the same time, the latter would have to be classed as a late work.[14] The careful choice of names to be given to children is a topic to which Chrysostom returns more than once. The nearest parallel to paragraph 47 of the address occurs in the twenty-first homily on Genesis, where the preacher observes: "Let us not then apply to our boys the first name that comes to hand nor yet bestow on them the names of grandfathers or great-grandfathers or persons distinguished for their birth, but rather the names of holy men, illustrious for virtue, men who have spoken freely with God." [15] Finally in paragraph 88 Chrysostom employs the striking metaphor of a chain which he likens to a series of Christian families, where each generation has been rightly brought up by the preceding generation. This metaphor is employed also in a homily which in other ways is very near in thought to the address. Fathers are concerned, he remarks, about giving their boys worldly possessions, but care nothing about their souls. Yet they should watch their sons' comings and goings with care, and their amusements and companions, in the knowledge that, if they are neglectful, God will not pardon them. Children are tender so that they can be molded and trained. Eli (I Samuel 2:12 ff.) was too indulgent to his sons. Exhortation is not enough. Fathers, because they are unwilling to flog or to reprove with words or to vex their boys when they are disorderly and lawless, may live to see the young men ruined, dragged to court, and executed. The father must remember that he has golden statues in his house, his children. They should be trained day by day and narrowly watched and their souls adorned. If a man train his boy correctly and the boy train his son correctly, and so on, the succession of good Christians will be like a chain.[16] It happens that this homily can be dated with great probability; it seems to have been delivered at Antioch in 388. The homilies on Genesis also belong to Chrysostom's Antiochene period. And so, of the three passages last quoted one belongs to the years when Chrysostom was metropolitan at Constantinople, two were written when he was still a priest in Antioch. We are driven to the conclusion that any theory which is built up on such internal evidence in order to date the address *On Vainglory* rests on flimsy foundations. Chrysostom kept his transcendent powers of speech to the end. His familiarity with the Bible and his vast store of *exempla* were never diminished. That he should reiterate the same views on an important subject at different periods of his life and even employ identical or very similar phrases and illustrations is surely not surprising. Has not every great speaker and preacher done the same?

An Address on Vainglory and the Right Way for Parents to Bring Up Their Children

BY JOHN CHRYSOSTOM

1. Has any man done what I asked? Has he prayed to
God on our behalf and on behalf of the whole body of
the Church for the quenching of the conflagration, be-
gotten of Vainglory,[1] which is bringing ruin on the entire
body of the Church and is tearing the single body asun-
der into many separate limbs and is disrupting love? Like
a wild beast swooping on a healthy, tender, and defense-
less body,[2] Vainglory has fastened her foul teeth in her
victim and injected poison and filled it with noisome
stench. She has severed and cast away some limbs, others
she has torn into shreds, others she has chewed up. Yea,
if it were possible to look on Vainglory and the Church
with our eyes, one would behold a pitiful sight, exceeding by far in savagery the spectacles in the circus—the
body of the Church prostrate and Vainglory standing over
it, gazing fixedly all round, restraining those that attack
her, never giving ground nor drawing back. Which of *us*
will scare away this wild beast? It is the task of Him who
has set the contest,[3] when we beseech Him to send his
angels, and they, muzzling her bold and shameless mouth
as it were with cords, lead her away so. He who has set the

[For notes to the translation, see pages 134–140.]

contest will do this whenever we cease to long for her when she has been led away. If He bids the dread beast withdraw from us and dismisses it, but we, after we have escaped safely and she has been driven off to her own den, rise up with our countless wounds and seek the beast once more and strike her and overturn her to carry her off, then He will pity us no longer nor spare us. "Who," saith one (Ecclesiasticus 12:13), "pitieth the charmer that is stung or any one that cometh nigh to a ravening beast?"

2. Well then? How may we be rid of this evil and wicked spirit? Truly it is a spirit with a lovely face. Suppose some spirit were to take on the form of a harlot [4] and, decking itself with many golden ornaments and putting on soft raiment and scenting itself with many perfumes, should steal into the semblance of a woman, a semblance most fair and concealing an exceeding beauty, and then should seem to be of that very age that most flutters the hearts of young men, with the bloom of youth upon her, encircled by a golden girdle and with curls on her head tastefully plaited in the Persian fashion; and should place a circlet about her head, enhancing the beauty of her uncovered tresses, and displaying flashing gold and precious gems about her throat; and the spirit, having assumed the shape of a youthful whore, should stand all alone before the brothel [5] and then should display the height of modesty. Whom of the youth that were there would she not capture? And then the spirit, leading the young man within the house, would put off that fair bloom and show itself in its own character, a hideous, fiery, savage spirit. And it would confound the wretched intruder and, leaping upon him and gaining possession of his soul, would drive his mind to frenzy. Even such is the wicked

spirit of Vainglory. Could anything seem fairer than her, anything more lovable? But if we see that it is all sham reality as in the theater, we shall not be ensnared in its nets nor caught by its stage tricks. The words spoken of a harlot (Proverbs 5:3) one might fairly utter also of such an one: "For the lips of a harlot woman drop as an honeycomb." The same word might truly be applied also to Vainglory.

3. Vainglory is like the fruit of Sodom,[6] which has a fair semblance and the beholder, as he views it, receives the impression of wholesome fruit. But if he takes in his hand a pomegranate or apple, straightway it is soft to his fingers and the rind that covers it outside is crushed and lets the fingers light upon dust and ashes. Such also is Vainglory. As we look upon her she seems tall and admirable, but when held fast in our hands forthwith she casts our soul down into the dust. That such is the nature of Vainglory can be proved by many examples. Well, then, let us begin, so you will, with the pagan world about us.

4. The theater is filling up,[7] and all the people are sitting aloft presenting a splendid sight and composed of numberless faces, so that many times the very rafters and roof above are hidden by human bodies. You can see neither tiles nor stones, but all is men's bodies and faces. Then, as the ambitious man who has brought them together enters in the sight of all, they stand up and as from a single mouth cry out. All with one voice call him protector and ruler of their common city and stretch out their hands in salutation. Next, betweenwhiles they liken him to the greatest of rivers, comparing his grand and lavish munificence to the copious waters of the Nile; and

they call him the Nile of gifts. Others, flattering him still more and thinking the simile of the Nile too mean, reject rivers and seas; and they instance the Ocean and say that he in his lavish gifts is what Ocean is among the waters, and they leave not a word of praise unsaid.[8] The face of Vainglory is brilliant, but do you recall, I pray, the likeness of the girl into which we fitted the evil spirit, decking it with gold and giving it the semblance of a youthful courtesan? And you will see that what is within the likeness is worthless.

5. What next? The great man bows to the crowd and in this way shows his regard. Then he sits down amid the congratulations of all his admirers, each of whom prays that he himself may attain to the same eminence and then die. But after a huge expenditure on gold, silver, horses, costumes, slaves, and the rest, and the waste of many fortunes, they greet his departure with the same eulogies, though there are no longer so many in the crowd; for, as the theater is ended, each man hastens to his own home. Then in his house there are costly luncheons and much feasting and the brilliance of daylight. In the afternoon the events of the morning are repeated, and this continues for two or three days. And so, when he has expended all, even to the value of ten thousand talents of gold, these words of praise are seen to be nought but embers, ashes, and dust.

6. As often as he examines the accounts in his household and reflects on the extravagant outlay, he laments. While he is enjoying his heart's desire he is possessed by a kind of intoxication of Vainglory and would expend himself as well, and he cannot form the smallest notion of his losses. But when he has come home—inside the

dwelling of this evil spirit—and sees that his hour of glory has departed as the concourse has dissolved, and he looks at the theater and finds it emptied of its audience and no man uttering a word, and that his losses are no thing of the imagination but have already been incurred in hard cash, then it is that he perceives the ashes.

7. And if, after he has spent beyond his fortune, he is in want, and standing on his feet begs in the center of the market place, and not one of those who formerly hailed him as their patron attends him or stretches out his hand, nay, what is more, if they rejoice at what has happened—for at the time when they hailed him, they were consumed with envy and thought it a consolation for their own domestic troubles that the man who had been so glorious was likely to be the most dishonored of all—when no man attends him or stretches out a hand, can anything be more pitiful than that? Nay, is it not rather deserving of tears? Could anything be more cruel?

8. Have you perhaps never at all heard of any man so unfortunate? One could wish that men had not stretched out their hands to him, but the opposite has happened; he is being assailed by the accusations of the very men who sang his praises. "Why," says one, "did he run riot? Why was he in love with splendor? for what reason did he gratify harlots and players?" Oh man without pity! Didst thou not marvel at him? Didst thou not sing his praise? Didst thou not lead him on to his present state by thy applause and flatteries? Didst thou not call him Nile and Ocean? Didst thou not spend all day in singing his praises? Whence thy sudden change of heart? And when pity is called for, dost thou accuse most bitterly those whom formerly thou didst applaud? If, when we

see a man being punished among those whom we accuse, we are not so stony-hearted as not to be moved, ought we not to be moved to pity all the more when we behold those in misfortune whom we belauded? But now thou art an accuser. When he gave thee pleasure with the spectacle, when thou didst pass the whole day neglecting all thy affairs, why didst thou not accuse him then?

9. Dost thou see of what kind are the Devil's works? Of what kind the fruits of Vainglory? I have called them ashes and dust. Nay, I see that they are not alone ashes and dust, but fire and smoke too; for the mischief does not stop at the point when enjoyment has ceased but endures until misfortunes overwhelm. It is ashes and dust for those who expend much and reap nothing, but it is so no less for those who suffer the misfortunes that I have just described.

10. "How then," someone says, "when the givers are honored for those public services and receive the admiration of the crowd, is that a small return?" Exceedingly small; for the honor that I have just described is not great—I mean, to be exposed to jeers and accusations and calumnies. "But what of those that receive honor?" The same is true; for they are honored not for the displays but because they are expected to spend further sums for the crowd. If they were honored for favors received, why do men accuse them when they have nothing? Why will men not even go near them but rather deride them and call them spendthrifts and profligates? Hast thou not seen that Vainglory is like a madness?

11. But let us leave this aspect of Vainglory which is found only in one or two men, and turn to another. Suppose someone says: "What of those who spend in modera-

tion on the amusements of the cities?" Tell me, I pray: What profits it? For them also the glory and the acclaim is but of a day. And to prove that this is so: Suppose someone gave them the choice of recovering all that money spent or a third part of it or even a small fraction, or else to have listened to no shouts of acclamation, dost thou think that they would not have preferred them ten thousand times? For if they commit ten thousand acts of shame and recklessness for a single obol, what would they not have done for all that money poured out at random?

12. At this point I direct my discourse to the faithful among us who refuse to hand over a trifling sum to Christ when He is poor and lacking the barest sustenance; and what the pagans spend on harlots and mimes and dancers in return for a single shout of applause, this our Christian will not give for the sake of the eternal kingdom.

13. But let us pass to another aspect of Vainglory. Which do I mean? One that affects many and not just one or two. We are pleased whenever men praise us even in respect of matters in which we are not implicated in the least degree. Now, the poor man does all he can to clothe himself in fine raiment for no other reason than that he may be held in honor by the crowd. And oftentimes, though he is able to do things for himself, he buys a slave, not because he needs him but that he may not appear disgraced by doing his own work. Tell me, for what reason dost thou, after relying so long on the labor of thine own hands, wish now to be served by the hands of others? Or again, if a man acquires gold besides and owns silver plate and a fine house? [9] He needs none of these possessions; for, if they were needed, the greater part of the human race would have perished and been

destroyed, as I will show you. There are necessities without which life is impossible; for example, the fruits of
the earth are necessary, and if the earth does not bear
life is impossible. Clothing to cover us, a roof and walls,
shoes—these belong to the necessities, but all other possessions are superfluous. If these also were needful and
a man could not live without a servant, as he cannot live
without those real necessities, the majority of mankind
would have perished, seeing that the majority has no
servants. If it were needful to make use of silver plate and
life without it were impossible, again the majority of mankind would have been destroyed, since the many do not
own silver either. Suppose someone says to the owners of
silver: "What does this plate mean to you?" The owner
could only give as his reason the honor paid him by the
crowd. "Well, I have acquired the plate so as to be admired and not looked down upon; but I hide it again, so
that men may not envy and threaten me." What could
be worse than folly of this kind? If thou ownest it that
the crowd may pay you honor, then display it for all to
see; but if thou fearest their envy, it is not good to own it
at all.

14. Shall I tell you another folly? Oftentimes men,
who have deprived themselves of the necessities and are
wasting with hunger, still care for their household possessions. And, if you ask them why, they answer: "I must
keep up my place." [10] What place, O man? Place does not
make a man's character. The righteous Elijah utterly
despised place, and Elisha too, and John. The first owned
nothing but a sheepskin and asked alms of a widow
woman, though she herself was poor; and he lived a beg-
gar's life, coming to the doorway of that poor woman and

uttering such words as beggars utter (I Kings 17:10 ff.). Elisha also despised place when he used to be the poor woman's guest (II Kings 4:8). John despised place since he had no garment nor a single loaf (Matthew 3:4; Mark 1:6). There is but one kind of place that is shameful, I mean the possession of great wealth, and that is shameful indeed. It brings a man the reputation of cruelty, effeminacy, lazy arrogance, vainglory, and brutality. Place consists not in wearing good raiment but in being clad in good works.

15. Yet I hear of many who are admired for this. "So and so," someone says, "takes thought for his place. His couch is spread and he has an abundance of bronze vessels; he is the manager of his own house." "And why," says another, "dost thou accuse us who own these things, when thou shouldst accuse those with greater possessions?" Through you I denounce them even more; for if I do not forbear from charging those who have little, how much more do I charge the wealthy. Place does not consist of a well-burnished house nor of costly tapestries nor a well-spread bed nor a decorated couch nor a crowd of servants. All these are externals and concern us not; but the things that concern us are fair dealing, disdain of money and fame, contempt for what the many think honor, disregard of human values, embracing poverty, and overcoming our nature by the virtue of our lives. It is these that constitute good place and reputation and honor. But what gives rise to all these evils from the beginning and the manner of it, I tell you now.

16. The man-child has lately been born. His father thinks of every means, not whereby he may direct the child's life wisely, but whereby he may adorn it and clothe

it in fine raiment and golden ornaments. Why dost thou this, O man? Granted that thou dost thyself wear these, why dost thou rear in this luxury thy son who is as yet still ignorant of this folly? For what purpose dost thou put a necklet about his throat? There is need for a strict tutor to direct the boy, no need for gold. And thou lettest his hair hang down behind, thereby at once making him look effeminate and like a girl and softening the ruggedness of his sex.[11] Implanting in him from the first an excessive love of wealth and teaching him to be excited by things of no profit, why dost thou plot even greater treachery against him? Why dost thou excite him with the pleasures of the body? "If a man have long hair," Paul says (I Corinthians 11:14), "it is a shame unto him." Nature disallows it, God has not sanctioned it, the thing is forbidden. It is an act of pagan superstition. Many also hang golden earrings on their children. Would that not even girls took pleasure in these; but you inflict this outrage on boys.

17. Many may laugh at what I am saying on the ground that these things are trifles. They are not trifles but of the first importance. The girl who has been reared in her mother's quarters to be excited by female ornaments, when she leaves her father's house will be a sore vexation to her bridegroom and a greater burden to him than the tax collectors.[12] I have told you already that vice is hard to drive away for this reason, that no one takes thought for his children, no one discourses to them about virginity and sobriety or about contempt of wealth and fame, or of the precepts laid down in the Scriptures.

18. What will become of boys when from earliest youth they are without teachers? If grown men, after being nurtured from the womb and continuing their education to

old age, still do not live righteously, what wrong will not children, accustomed from the threshold of life to empty words, commit? In our own day every man takes the greatest pains to train his boy in the arts and in literature and speech. But to exercise this child's soul in virtue, to that no man any longer pays heed.[13]

19. I shall not cease exhorting and begging and supplicating you before all else to discipline your sons from the first. If thou dost care for thy son, show it thus, and in other ways too thou wilt have thy reward. Hearken to the words of Paul, "if they continue in faith and charity and holiness with sobriety" (I Timothy 2:15). And even if thou art conscious of a myriad vices within thyself, nevertheless devise some compensation for thy vices. Raise up an athlete for Christ![14] I do not mean by this, hold him back from wedlock and send him to desert regions and prepare him to assume the monastic life. It is not this that I mean. I wish for this and used to pray that all might embrace it; but as it seems to be too heavy a burden, I do not insist upon it. Raise up an athlete for Christ and teach him though he is living in the world to be reverent from his earliest youth.

20. If good precepts are impressed on the soul while it is yet tender,[15] no man will be able to destroy them when they have set firm, even as does a waxen seal. The child is still trembling and fearful and afraid in look and speech and in all else. Make use of the beginning of his life as thou shouldst. Thou wilt be the first to benefit, if thou hast a good son, and then God. Thou dost labor for thyself.

21. They say that pearls when first they are collected are but water.[16] But if he that receives them is skilled in his craft, he places the drop on his hand; and, moving it with a

gentle rotating movement as it lies on the palm of his up-turned hand, he shapes it skillfully and renders it perfectly round. Then, when it has received its form, he can no longer mold it; for that which is soft and with its proper shape not yet set firm is in every way adaptable and therefore is easily suited to every purpose. But that which is hard, having acquired a certain material outline, can be deprived of its hardness only with difficulty and is not changed into another shape.

22. To each of you fathers and mothers I say, just as we see artists fashioning their paintings and statues with great precision, so we must care for these wondrous statues of ours. Painters when they have set the canvas on the easel paint on it day by day to accomplish their purpose.[17] Sculptors, too, working in marble, proceed in a similar manner; they remove what is superfluous and add what is lacking. Even so must you proceed. Like the creators of statues do you give all your leisure to fashioning these wondrous statues for God. And, as you remove what is superfluous and add what is lacking, inspect them day by day, to see what good qualities nature has supplied so that you will increase them, and what faults so that you will eradicate them. And, first of all, take the greatest care to banish licentious speech; for love of this above all frets the souls of the young. Before he is of an age to try it, teach thy son to be sober and vigilant and to shorten sleep for the sake of prayer, and with every word and deed to set upon himself the seal of the faith.[18]

23. Regard thyself as a king ruling over a city which is the soul of thy son; for the soul is in truth a city.[19] And, even as in a city some are thieves and some are honest men, some work steadily and some transact their business fit-

fully, so it is with the thoughts and reasoning in the soul. Some make war on wrongdoers, like soldiers in a city; others take thought for everything, both the welfare of the body and of the home, like those who carry on the government in cities. Some give orders, like the magistrates, some again counsel lewdness, like profligates, others reverence, like the virtuous. And some are effeminate, even as are women among us; others speak folly, like children. And some again receive orders as slaves, like servants in the city, while others are wellborn, like free men.

24. Hence we need laws to banish evildoers and admit the good and prevent the evildoers from rising up against the good. And, just as in a city, if laws are passed which permit thieves great license, the general welfare is undermined, and if the soldiers do not devote their ardor to its proper use, they ruin the body politic, and if each citizen abandons his own household affairs and busies himself with another's, he destroys good order by his greed and ambition—so it is also in the case of the child.

25. The child's soul then is a city, a city but lately founded and built, a city containing citizens who are strangers with no experience as yet, such as it is very easy to direct; for men who have been reared and have grown old under a bad constitution it would be difficult to reform, though not impossible. Even they can be reformed if they be willing. But those who are quite without experience would readily accept the laws that thou givest them.

26. Draw up laws then for this city and its citizens, laws that inspire fear and are strong, and uphold them if they are being transgressed; for it is useless to draw up laws, if their enforcement does not follow.

27. Draw up laws, and do you pay close attention; for

our legislation is for the world and today we are founding a city. Suppose that the outer walls and four gates, the senses, are built. The whole body shall be the wall, as it were, the gates are the eyes, the tongue, the hearing, the sense of smell, and, if you will, the sense of touch. It is through these gates that the citizens of the city go in and out; that is to say, it is through these gates that thoughts are corrupted or rightly guided.

28. Well now, let us first of all approach the gate of the tongue, seeing that this is the busiest of all; and let us, to begin with and before all the other gates, provide this one with doors and bolts, not of wood or iron but of gold. Verily the city that is thus equipped is golden; for it is not any mortal but the King of the universe who intends to dwell in this city, if it has been well built. And, as our discourse proceeds, you shall see where we set up His palace. So let us build for the city gates and bolts of gold, that is, the words of God, even as the prophet says (Psalms 118 [119]: 103; 18 [19]:10): "The words of God are sweeter than honey and honeycomb to my mouth, more precious than gold and a stone of great price." Let us teach the child so that the words revolve on his lips all the time, even on his walks abroad, not lightly nor incidentally nor at rare intervals, but without ceasing. It is not enough merely to cover the gates with gold leaf. They must be fashioned of gold thick and solid through and through, and they must have precious stones set well in instead of merely laid on the surface. The bolt of these gates shall be the Cross of the Lord fashioned through and through of precious gems and set athwart the middle of the gates. But when we have fashioned the gates massive and golden and have fixed on the bolt, we must fashion the citizens also to be worthy of

the city. Of what character shall these citizens be? We must train the child to utter grave and reverent words. We must drive many strangers away, so that no corrupt men may also find their way in to mingle with these citizens. Words that are insolent and slanderous, foolish, shameful, common, and worldly, all these we must expel. And no one save only the King must pass through these gates (cf. Ezekiel 44:2). For Him and all that are His this gate shall be open so that one may say of it (Psalms 117 [118]:20): "This is the gate of the Lord into which the righteous shall enter," and, as the blessed Paul says (Ephesians 4:29),[20] "speech that is good for edifying, that it may minister grace unto the hearers." Let their words be giving thanks, solemn hymns; let their discourse ever be about God, about heavenly philosophy.

29. How shall this be? And in what manner shall we train them? If we are zealous critics of those that are growing. The boy is very easily guided. He does not fight for wealth or glory—he is still a small boy—nor on behalf of wife or children or home. What reason for insolence or evil-speaking should he have? He contends only with companions of his own age.

30. Make a law straightway that he use no one in despite, that he speak ill of no man, that he swear not, that he be not contentious. If thou shouldst see him transgressing this law, punish him, now with a stern look, now with incisive, now with reproachful, words; at other times win him with gentleness and promises. Have not recourse to blows constantly and accustom him not to be trained by the rod; for if he feel it constantly as he is being trained, he will learn to despise it. And when he has learnt to despise it, he has reduced thy system to nought. Let him rather at all times fear blows

but not receive them.[21] Threaten him with the tawse, but do not lay it on and do not let thy threats proceed to action. Do not let it appear that thy words do not pass the stage of threats; for a threat is only of use when attended by the belief that it will be put into effect. If the offender learn your intention, he will despise it. So let him expect chastisement but not receive it, so that his fear may not be quenched but may endure, like a raging fire drawing thorny brushwood from every side or like a sharp and searching pick digging to the very depths. Yet when thou dost see that he has profited by fear, forbear, seeing that our human nature has need of some forbearance.

31. Teach him to be fair and courteous. If thou dost see a servant ill-used by him, do not overlook it, but punish him who is free; for if he knows that he may not ill use even a slave, he will abstain all the more from insulting or slandering one who is free and of his class. Stop his mouth from speaking evil. If thou dost see him traducing another, curb him and direct his tongue toward his own faults.

32. Exhort his mother, too, to converse with the child thus, and his tutor and his servant, so all of them together may be his guardians and on the watch that none of those evil thoughts spring out from the boy and from that mouth and from the golden gates.

33. And do not, I pray, think that this takes a long time. If from the first thou dost firmly lay on thy behests and threats and dost appoint so many guardians, two months suffice, and all is in good order and the habit is firmly established as his second nature.

34. Thus this gate will have been made worthy of the Lord, when no word that is shameful or flippant or foolish or the like is spoken, but all beseems the Master. If those

who give military training teach their sons from the first to be soldiers and to shoot and to put on military dress and to ride, and their tender years are no hindrance, how much more should those who are soldiers of God assume all this royal discipline. So let him learn to sing hymns to God that he may not spend his leisure on shameful songs and ill-timed tales.

35. Let this gate thus be made secure and let these be the citizens that are enrolled. But the others within the city let us put to death, as bees kill drones, and let us not allow them to sally forth or buzz.

36. Now let us pass to another gate. Which is that? One that lies close by the first and resembles it greatly, I mean, the sense of hearing. The first gate has citizens that go forth from within, and none that enter in by it; but this second gate has only those that enter in from outside, none that pass out through it. The second then much resembles the first. If it be agreed that none that is pernicious and corrupt may tread upon its threshold, the mouth experiences but little trouble; for he that hears no base or wicked words does not utter base words either. But if this gate stands wide open to all, the other will suffer harm and all those within will be thrown into confusion. And it was needful to speak fully about the former gate and first to block up its entrance.

37. Let children then hear nothing harmful from servants or tutor or nurses. But, even as plants need the greatest amount of care when they are tender shoots, so also do children; and so let us take thought for good nurses that a fair foundation from the ground up be laid for the young and that from the beginning they may receive nought that is evil.

38. Therefore let them not hear frivolous and old wives' tales: "This youth kissed that maiden. The king's son and the younger daughter have done this." [22] Do not let them hear these stories, but let them hear others simply told with no elaboration. They can hear such from slaves but not from all. They must not be allowed to consort with all the servants, but rather let those who are participating with us in training stand out clearly, as though they were approaching a holy statue. If we were builders and were erecting a house for the ruler, we should not permit one and all of the servants to approach the building. Would it not then be absurd, when we are establishing a city and citizens for the heavenly King, to entrust the task indiscriminately to all? Let those of the servants who are well fitted take part. If there be none, then hire someone who is free, a virtuous man, and entrust the task especially to him, so that he may have a full share in the undertaking.

39. Let them not hear such tales. But when the boy takes relaxation from his studies—for the soul delights to dwell on stories of eld— [23] speak to him, drawing him away from all childish folly; for thou art raising a philosopher and athlete and citizen of heaven. Speak to him and tell him this story: "Once upon a time there were two sons of one father, even two brothers." Then after a pause continue: "And they were the children of the same mother, one being the elder, the other the younger son. The elder was a tiller of the ground, the younger a shepherd; and he led out his flocks to woodland and lake." Make thy stories agreeable that they may give the child pleasure and his soul may not grow weary. "The other son sowed and planted. And it came to pass that both wished to do honor to God. And the shepherd took the firstlings of his flocks and offered them

to God." Is it not a far better thing to relate this than fairy tales about sheep with golden fleeces? Then arouse him—for not a little depends on the telling of the story—introducing nothing that is untrue but only what is related in the Scriptures: "Now when he offered the firstlings to God, straightway fire came down from heaven and bore them off to the altar aloft. But the elder son did not so but went away and, after storing up for himself the first fruits from his toil, brought the second-best to God. And God paid no heed to them but turned away and let them lie on the ground. But the other offering he received for himself in heaven. Even so it happens with earthly rulers. The master honors one who brings gifts and receives him in his house; another he suffers to stand outside. Even so it was in this story. And then what happened? The elder brother was very wroth as having been dishonored and passed over for another, and his countenance fell. God said unto him: 'Why art thou wroth? Didst thou not know that thou madest an offering to God? Why hast thou insulted me? What grievance hast thou? Why didst thou offer me the second-best?' " If it seems well to use simpler language, thou wilt say: "The elder brother had nothing to say and kept quiet," or better, "was silent. And thereafter, seeing his younger brother, he said to him: 'Let us go to the field.' And the elder caught the younger unawares and slew him. And he thought that God saw him not. But God came to him and said to him: 'Where is thy brother?' He replied: 'I know not. Am I my brother's keeper?' And God said unto him: 'Lo, the voice of thy brother's blood crieth unto me from the ground.' "

And let the child's mother sit by while his soul is being formed thus by such tales, so that she too may take part and praise the story. "What happened next? God received the younger son into heaven; having died he is up above." The child also learns the story of raising from the dead. If in pagan legend such marvels are told, one says: 'He made the soul the soul of a hero.' And the child believes and, while he does not know what a hero is, he knows that it is something greater than a man. And as soon as he hears, he marvels. Much more will he do so when he hears of raising from the dead and that the younger brother's soul went up to heaven. "And so God received the one straightway; but the other, the slayer, lived for many years continuously in misfortune, with fear and trembling as his companions, and suffered ten thousand ills and was punished every day." And do thou relate the punishment with much intensity and not simply that he heard God say: 'Groaning and trembling thou shalt be on the earth'; for the child does not understand this yet. But say: "Just as thou, when thou art standing before thy teacher and art in an agony of doubt whether thou art to receive a whipping, thou tremblest and art afraid, even so did he live all his days, because he had given offense to God."

40. So far is enough for the child. Tell him this story one evening at supper. Let his mother repeat the same tale; then, when he has heard it often, ask him too, saying: "Tell me the story," so that he may be eager to imitate you. And when he has memorized it thou wilt also tell him how it profits him. The soul indeed, as it receives the story within itself before thou hast elaborated it, is aware that it will benefit. Nevertheless, do thou say hereafter: "Thou dost see how great a sin is greed, how great a sin it is to envy a brother. Thou dost see how great a sin it is to think that thou canst hide aught from God; for He sees all things,

even those that are done in secret." If only thou sowest the
seed of this teaching in the child, he will not need his tutor,
since this fear that comes from God, this complete fear has
possessed the boy instead and shakes his soul.

41. This is not all. Go leading him by the hand in church
and pay heed particularly when this tale is read aloud.
Thou wilt see him rejoice and leap with pleasure because
he knows what the other children do not know, as he an-
ticipates the story, recognizes it, and derives great gain
from it. And hereafter the episode is fixed in his memory.

42. He can profit in other ways from the story. So let him
learn from thee: "There is no reason for grief in adversity.
God shows this from the very first in the example of this
boy, seeing that He received one who was righteous
through death into heaven."

43. When this story is firmly planted in the child's understanding, introduce another, again about two brothers,
and speak thus: "Again there were two brothers, an elder
and a younger. The elder was a hunter, the younger dwelt
at home." Now this story, insofar as the reversal of fortune
is greater [24] and the brothers are older, gives more pleasure
than the former one. "Now these two brothers were also
twins. And after their birth the mother loved the younger,
the father the elder son. Now the elder passed much of his
time out of doors in the fields, but the younger indoors.
And it came to pass when his father was old, that he said
to the son whom he loved: 'My son, I am old. Go thou and
prepare me some game, capture a roe or a hare and bring it
and cook it that I may eat and bless thee.' But to the
younger son he spoke no such words. But his mother heard
what the father had said and called her younger son and
said unto him: 'Child, thy father has bidden thy brother

bring to him game that he may eat and bless him. Hearken to me and go to the flock and fetch me fair and tender kids, and I will prepare them as thy father loveth, and thou shalt carry them to him that he may eat and bless thee.' Now the father's eyes were dim from old age. And so when the younger son brought the kids, his mother seethed them, and placing the viands on the dish gave it to her son, and he bore it in. And she put the skin of the goats upon him that he might not be found out, since his skin was smooth but his brother was hairy, so that the younger might escape detection and his father perceive it not. And so she sent him in. But the father, thinking that it was in truth his elder son, ate and gave him his blessing. But then, as soon as the father had made an end of the blessing, the elder son came bringing game; and when he saw what had happened, he lifted up his voice and wept."

44. See how many fair lessons this story begets, and do not follow it right through to the end, but rather see how many lessons this part begets. First, children learn to reverence and honor their fathers, when they see so keen a rivalry for the father's blessing. And they will sooner suffer a myriad stripes than to hear their parents curse them. If a story can so master the children's soul that it is thought worthy of belief, the veritable truth, it will surely enthrall them and fill them with great awe. Again, they must learn to despise the belly; for the story must also show them that he gained nothing by being first-born and the elder. Because of the greed of his belly he betrayed the advantage of his birthright.

45. Then, when the boy has grasped this fully, thou wilt say to him again on another evening: "Tell me the story of those two brothers." And if he begins to relate the story of

Cain and Abel, stop him and say: "It is not that one that I want, but the one of the other brothers, in which the father gave his blessing." Give him hints but do not as yet tell him their names. When he has told you all, spin the sequel of the yarn, and say:

46. "Hear what occurred afterwards. Once again the elder brother, like the brother in the former story, was minded to slay his brother, and he was awaiting his father's death. But their mother hearing him and being fearful sent the younger into exile." Then, as the inward sense transcends the child's intelligence,[25] it can be simplified to his level of understanding and implanted in this tender childish intelligence, if we adapt the tale. And we shall speak to him thus: "This brother went away and came to a certain place. And he had no one with him, no slave or nurse or tutor or anyone else. And having come to a certain place he prayed, saying: 'Lord, give me bread and raiment and preserve me.' And then, when he had spoken thus, he fell asleep from sorrow. And in a dream he saw a ladder reaching from the earth to heaven and the angels of God ascending and descending on it and God Himself standing above at the head of the ladder; and he said, 'Give me Thy blessing.' And He blessed him and named him Israel."

47. I have remembered opportunely, and the name suggests another notion to my mind. What is this? Let us afford our children from the first an incentive to goodness from the name that we give them. Let none of us hasten to call his child after his forebears, his father and mother and grandsire and great-grandsire, but rather after the righteous—martyrs, bishops, apostles. Let this be an incentive to the children. Let one be called Peter, another John, another bear the name of one of the saints.[26]

48. And do not, I pray, follow Greek customs. It is a great disgrace and laughable when in a Christian household some Greek pagan customs are observed; and they kindle lamps and sit watching to see which is the first to be extinguished and consumed, and other such customs which bring certain destruction to those who practice them. Do not regard such doings as paltry and trivial.[27]

49. And so I urge this on you too, to call your children by the names of the righteous. In early times these other customs were reasonable, and men used to call their children by the names of their forebears. It was a consolation for death that the departed should seem to live through his name.[28] But this is so no longer. We see at least that the righteous did not name their children in this wise. Abraham begat Isaac. Jacob and Moses were not called after their forebears, and we shall not find a single one of the righteous who was named so. How great is the virtue of which this is a token, this naming and calling by name, seeing that we shall find no other reason for the change of name save that it brings virtue to mind. "Thou shalt be called Cephas," says Christ (John 1:42), "which is by interpretation Peter." Why? Because thou didst acknowledge me. And thou shalt be called Abraham. Why? Because thou shalt be the father of nations (Genesis 17: 4). And Israel, because he saw God (cf. Genesis 35:9–10). And so let us begin the care and training of our children from that point.

50. But as I was relating: "He saw a ladder extended and reaching up to heaven." So let the name of the saints enter our homes through the naming of our children, to train not only the child but the father, when he reflects that he is the father of John or Elijah or James; for, if the name be given with forethought to pay honor to those that have

departed, and we grasp at our kinship with the righteous rather than with our forebears, this too will greatly help us and our children. Do not because it is a small thing regard it as small; its purpose is to succour us.

51. But as I was saying, let us return to the sequel of the story: "He saw a ladder firmly planted. He craved a blessing. God blessed him. He departed to his kinsmen. He was a shepherd." Relate further the story of his bride and his return home, and the boy will profit much therefrom. Consider how many things he will learn. He will be trained to trust in God, to despise no one though the son of one who is wellborn, to feel no shame at simple thrift, to bear misfortune nobly, and all the rest.

52. Next, when he has grown older, tell him also more fearful tales; for thou shouldst not impose so great a burden on his understanding while he is still tender, lest thou dismay him. But when he is fifteen years old or more, let him hear of Hell. Nay, when he is ten or eight or even younger, let him hear in full detail the story of the flood, the destruction of Sodom, the descent into Egypt—whatever stories are full of divine punishment. When he is older let him hear also the deeds of the New Testament—deeds of grace and deeds of hell. With these stories and ten thousand others fortify his hearing, as thou dost offer him also examples drawn from his home.

53. But if any man would relate what is base, let us not, as I have said, suffer him to come near the boy. If thou dost see a slave in his presence speaking lewdly, punish him straightway and inquire zealously and sharply into the offense committed. If thou dost see a girl—but better by far that no woman, save it be some time an old woman with no charms to captivate a youth, come near him and

the flame of desire be not kindled. But from a young woman shield him as from fire.[29] In this way then he will speak no foolish word, if he hears nought that is foolish but is brought up on those stories that we have told.

54. Let us pass on, if thou wilt, to another gate, the sense of smell. This gate too admits much that is harmful if it be not kept barred—I mean fragrant scents and herbs. Nothing weakens, nothing relaxes the right tension of the soul as a pleasure in sweet odors.[30] "How then," says some one, "must one take pleasure in filth?" That is not my meaning, but that one should not take pleasure either in the one or in the other. Let no one bring him perfume; for, as soon as it penetrates to the brain, the whole body is relaxed. Thereby pleasures are fanned into flame and great schemes for their attainment. So bar this gate, for its function is to breathe the air, not to receive sweet odors. It may be that some laugh at us for troubling about trifles, if we discourse about such a commonwealth. These are no trifles; nay, if we carry out our plan, our concern is with the origin and rhythmical education of the world.

55. Then there is yet another gate, fairer than those others but difficult to guard, the gate of the eyes; difficult for this reason, that it lies high up and open and is beautiful. It has many little postern gates and not only sees but is seen if well fashioned.

56. Here strict laws are needed, the first being: Never send thy son to the theater that he may not suffer utter corruption through his ears and eyes. And when he is abroad in the open squares, his attendant must be especially watchful as he passes through the alleys and must warn the boy of this, so that he may never suffer this corruption.

57. That he may not suffer it by his own appearance must have our careful thought. We must remove the chief part of his physical charm by clipping the locks on his head all round to attain severe simplicity. If the boy complain because he is being deprived of this charm, let him learn first of all that the greatest charm is simplicity.

58. That he may avoid seeing what he should not, those tales are sufficient protection which tell of "the sons of God that lapsed by coming in unto the daughters of men" (Genesis 6:4), and of the people of Sodom, of Gehenna, and the rest.[31]

59. In this matter the tutor and attendant must exercise the greatest care. Show the boy other fair sights, and thou wilt steer his eyes away from those others. Show him the sky, the sun, the flowers of the earth, meadows, and fair books.[32] Let these give pleasure to his eyes; and there are many others that are harmless.

60. This gate is difficult to guard, since there burns a fire within and, so to speak, a natural compulsion. Let him learn hymns. If he is not inwardly aroused, he will not wish to see outwardly. Let him not bathe in company with women—such familiarity is evil—and let him not be sent into a crowd of women.[33]

61. Let him hear the whole story of Joseph continually.[34] Furthermore, let him learn of the kingdom of Heaven and the great reward that awaits those who live sober lives. Promise him also that thou wilt lead to him a fair maid and tell him that thou hast made him the heir of thy property. Do not spare thy threats, if thou dost see the contrary disposition in him, and say to him: "My son, we shall not light upon a virtuous woman unless thou hast shown great watchfulness and devotion to virtue. And that thou may-

est be steadfast, I shall soon guide thee to marriage."

62. Above all, if he is trained to speak no shameful word, he has a firm foundation of reverence derived from above. Speak to him of the beauty of the soul, instil into him a resolute spirit against womankind. Say that to be despised by the slave woman is meet only for a slave, and that a young man has the greatest need of earnestness. He who speaks will be conspicuous, he who sees will not be conspicuous; for this sense is swift and, as he sits among many, he can pick what maid he wishes with quick glances.[35] Let him have no converse with any woman save only his mother. Let him see no woman. Do not give him money, let nothing shameful come in his way. Let him despise luxury and everything of that kind.

63. There is yet another gateway, unlike the others because it extends through the whole body. We call it touch. It appears to be closed, yet it is, as it were, open and sends within whatever comes. Let us not allow it to have any truck with soft raiment or bodies. Let us make it austere. We are raising an athlete, let us concentrate our thought on that. And so let him not use soft couches or raiment. Let these be our ordinances.

64. Come now, when we have entered this city, let us write down and ordain laws, seeing that our arrangement of the gates is so fair. First, let us thoroughly inform ourselves about the houses and chambers of the citizens that we may know where dwell the zealous and where the effete.

65. The seat and habitation of spirit, we are told, are the breast and the heart within the breast; of the appetitive part of the soul, the liver; of the reasoning part, the brain.[36] Spirit produces both good and bad qualities; the good are

sobriety and equability, the bad, rashness and ill temper. So, too, with the appetitive part; the good it causes is sobriety, the evil, licentiousness. And with the rational part the good is understanding, the bad, folly. Let us then have a care that the good qualities come to birth in these places and that they bear citizens of like character and not evil. These properties of the soul have been established to be like the mothers of our rational thoughts.

66. Let us pass to the despotic part of the soul, spirit. We must not eliminate it utterly from the youth nor yet allow him to use it all the time. Let us train boys from earliest childhood to be patient when they suffer wrongs themselves, but, if they see another being wronged, to sally forth courageously and aid the sufferer in fitting measure.

67. How shall we attain this? If they practice themselves among their own slaves and are patient when slighted and refrain from anger when they are disobeyed, but narrowly examine the faults that they themselves have committed against others. The father is arbiter at all times in such matters. If the laws are transgressed, he will be stern and unyielding; if they are observed, he will be gracious and kind and will bestow many rewards on the boy. Even so God rules the world with the fear of Hell and the promise of His Kingdom. So must we too rule our children.

68. And let there be many on all sides to spur the boy on, so that he may be exercised and practiced in controlling his passions among the members of the household. And, just as athletes in the wrestling school train with their friends before the contest, so that when they have succeeded against these they may be invincible against their opponents, even so the boy must be trained in the home. Let his father or brother oftentimes play the chief part in

treating him with despite. And let them all strive their hardest to overcome him. Or let someone in wrestling stand up to him and defend himself so that the boy may try his strength against him. So, too, let the slaves provoke him often rightly or wrongly, so that he may learn on every occasion to control his passion. If his father provoke him, it is no great test; for the name of father, taking first possession of his soul, does not permit him to rebel. But let his companions in age, whether slave or free, do this, that he may learn equability amongst them.

69. There is still another method. What is that? When he becomes angry, remind him of the lessons that he has learned at home. When he is wroth with his slave, if he himself has not committed a fault, remind him that he should behave as he would have done on those former occasions. If thou dost see him striking the slave, demand satisfaction for this, and do likewise if thou dost see him using the slave ill. Let him be neither indulgent nor harsh, that he may be both a man and equable. Oftentimes he needs the help that spirit can give, as would be the case if at some time he himself have children or be the master of slaves. At all times the faculty of spirit is serviceable; it is only unprofitable when we defend ourselves. For this reason also Paul never made use of it for himself but only for others who had suffered wrong. And Moses, seeing his brother wronged, was wroth, and that right nobly, although he was "the meekest of men" (Exodus 2:11 ff.). But when he was used despitefully, he no longer defended himself but fled. Let the boy hear these tales. When we are still engaged in ordering the gates, we need the more artless stories; when we have entered in and are training the citizens, then is the time for those of a loftier kind. And so, let this be his first law, never

to defend himself when ill used or suffering misfortune, and never to allow another to undergo this.

70. The father, if he discipline himself also, will be far better in teaching the boy these precepts; for, if for no other reason, he will improve himself so as not to spoil the example that he sets. Let the boy be taught to suffer despite and contumely. Let him not demand from the servants such services as a free man demands, but for the most part let him minister to his own needs. Let the slaves only render such services as he cannot do for himself. A free man, for example, cannot do his own cooking; for he must not devote himself to such pursuits at the cost of neglecting the labors befitting a free man. If, however, the boy would wash his feet, never let a slave do this, but let him do it for himself. Thus thou wilt render the free man considerate toward his slaves and greatly beloved by them. Do not let a slave hand him his cloak, and do not let him expect another to serve him in the bath, but let him do all these things for himself. This will make him strong and simple and courteous.

71. Teach him the facts of natural society and the difference between slave and free man.[37] Say to him: "My son, there were no slaves of old in the time of our forebears, but sin brought slavery in its train; for when one insulted his father, he paid this penalty, to become his brothers' bondsman (Genesis 9:21–25). Beware lest thou be the slave of thy slaves. If thou art wroth and thy conduct is the same as theirs and thou art no whit more virtuous than they, thou wilt earn no greater respect than they. Strive therefore to be their master and become so, not by doing as they do, but by thy habits, so that being a free man thou art never a slave of these. Dost thou not see how many fathers have

renounced their sons and have introduced slaves in their place? Look then that no such thing happens to you. Truly I neither wish nor desire it, but the choice lies with you."

72. In this way dispose his spirit to gentleness and bid him treat his servants like brothers, and teach him the facts of natural society, quoting to him the words of Job (31:13–15): "If I did despise the cause of my manservant or of my maidservant, when they contended with me; what shall I do when God afflicteth me and when he visiteth, what shall I answer him? Did not he that made me in the womb make them? Were we not fashioned in the same womb?" And again: "If my maidservants said often, 'who would give us of his flesh to be satisfied,' since I am too kindly." [38]

73. Or dost thou think Paul a simpleton for saying that one who knows not how to rule his own house cannot superintend the church either (I Timothy 3:5)? [39] So say to the boy: "If thou dost see that thy servant has destroyed one of thy pencils or broken a pen, be not angry or abusive but forgiving and placable. Thus taught by small losses thou wilt learn to bear the greater. Or it might be the strap about your writing tablets or the bronze chain that is broken." Children are made fractious by the loss of such articles and incline rather to lose their soul than to let the culprit go unpunished. There then one must soften the asperity of his anger. Believe me, the boy who is indifferent to such things and placable will endure every loss when he becomes a man. So if the boy has tablets fashioned of fine wood, clean and without stain, held together by bronze chains, and silver pencils and other like boyish possessions, and his servant lose or break them, and then the boy refrain from anger, he has displayed already all the marks of a

philosophic mind. Do not straightway buy him others, lest you abate his sufferings; but when you see that he no longer misses his loss or is distressed by it, then heal his misfortune.

74. I am not speaking of trifles, we are discussing the governance of the world. Train the boy also, if he has a younger brother, to let him take precedence or, if not, his servant; for this also involves a philosophical disposition.

75. Mold his spirit so that it begets rational thoughts that are friendly to us. When he is dependent on no one, when he suffers loss, when he needs no service, when he does not resent honor paid to another, what source will there be left for anger?

76. It is now time to pass to desire. Both the self-restraint and the harm involved are twofold, that he may not himself suffer outrage nor yet himself do outrage to girls. The medical guild [40] tell us that this desire attacks with violence after the fifteenth year. How shall we tie down this wild beast? What shall we contrive? How shall we place a bridle on it? I know none, save only the restraint of hell-fire.

77. First then let us guide it away from shameful spectacles and songs. Never let a free-born boy enter the theater.[41] If he yearn after the pleasure to be found there, let us point out any of his companions who are holding back from this, so that he may be held fast in the grip of emulation. Nothing, yea nothing, is so effective as emulation. Let us act thus in every instance, especially if he be emulous; for this is a more potent instrument than fear or promises or ought else.

78. Next, let us devise for him other harmless pleasures. Let us lead him to saintly men, let us give him recreation, let us show our regard for him by many gifts, so that his

soul may patiently bear our rejection of the theater. In place of those spectacles introduce pleasing stories, flowery meadows, and fair buildings. And thereafter let us overthrow those spectacles by our argument, as we say to him: "My child, spectacles such as those, the sight of naked women uttering shameful words, are for slaves. Promise me not to listen to or speak any unseemly word and go thy way. There it is impossible not to hear what is base; what goes on is unworthy of thy eyes." As we speak to him, let us kiss him and put our arms about him, and press him to us to show our affection. By all these means let us mold him.

79. Well then, as I said before, never allow any maid to approach him or to serve him, save it be a slave of advancing years, an old woman. And let us guide the conversation to the kingdom of heaven and to those men of old, pagan or Christian, who were illustrious for their self-restraint.[42] Let us constantly flood his ears with talk of them. If we should also have servants of sober conduct, let us draw comparisons also from them, saying how absurd to have so sober a servant, while the free man is inferior to him in conduct. There is another remedy yet. Which is that? Let him also learn to fast, not indeed all the while, but on two days of the week, on Wednesday and Friday.[43] Let him visit the church. And let the father take the boy in the evening when the theater is ended and point to the spectators coming out and make fun of the older men because they have less sense than the young and the young men because they are inflamed with desire. And let him ask the boy: "What have all these people gained? Nothing but shame, reproach, and damnation." Abstention from all these spectacles and songs conduces not a little to virtue.

80. Furthermore, let him learn to pray with great fervor and contrition; and do not tell me that a lad would never conform to these practices. Certainly the lad would conform to them if he were keen-eyed and wide-awake. We see many examples of it among the men of old, for instance, Daniel or Joseph. And do not speak to me of Joseph's seventeen years and consider first why he won his father's love, and that more than the older sons. Was not Jacob younger than he? or Jeremiah? Was not Daniel twelve years of age? Was not Solomon himself but twelve when he prayed that wondrous prayer (I Kings 3:6–9)? Did not Samuel when still young instruct his own teacher (I Samuel 3:17)? So let us not despair; for one who is too immature in soul does not conform even when he is an adult. Let the boy be trained to pray with much contrition and to keep vigils as much as he is able, and let the stamp of a saintly man be impressed on the boy in every way. If he refrains from oaths,[44] and from insults when he is insulted, and from slander and hatred, and if he fasts and prays, all this is a sufficient guide to virtue.

81. If thou dost bring him up to the secular life, introduce his bride to him straightway and do not wait for him to be a soldier or engage in political life before you do so.[45] First train his soul and then take thought for his reputation in the world. Or dost thou think the fact of a virgin youth and a virgin maid being united is a trifling contribution to their marriage? It is no trifle, not only for the virtue of the youth but for the maiden's also. Will not then the charm of their love be wholly pure? Above all, will not God then be the more gracious and fill that marriage with countless blessings, when they come together according to His ordi-

nances? And He makes the youth remember his love always. And if he is held fast in this affection, he will spurn every other woman.

82. If thou dost sing the maiden's praise for her beauty and her comeliness and all the rest, adding that "she will not endure to be thy mate if she learns that thou art slothful," he will reflect deeply, seeing that his ultimate happiness is imperiled. If love of the betrothed induced the holy patriarch after he had been deceived to serve for a second term of seven years, to serve for fourteen in all (Genesis 29:20–30), how much more must we. Say to him: "All that know thy bride—her father and mother, her servants and neighbors and friends—are deeply concerned for thee and thy way of life, and all will report to her." Bind him then with this fetter, the fetter that makes virtue secure. Then, even if he cannot have a wife from his earliest manhood, let him have a betrothed from the first and let him strive to show himself a good man. This is enough safeguard to ward off every evil.

83. There is yet another protection of virtue. Let him often see the head of his church and let him hear many words of praise from the bishop's lips; and let his father pride himself on this before all the hearers. Let the maidens as they see him be filled with awe; and so the tales and the fear of his father and his promises; and with these the reward laid up for him from God, even the numerous blessings which the virtuous shall enjoy—all this will afford him great security.

84. Refer also to distinctions won in the army and in political life; and, besides, at all times express contempt for lewdness and give abundant praise for self-restraint. All

these things serve to restrain the boy's soul; and so we shall find them giving birth to serious reflections.

85. There is something more. Let us go to the master principle which keeps everything under control. To what do I allude? I mean wisdom. Here great labor is needed to render him sagacious and to banish all folly. This is the great and wondrous function of philosophy, that he may know God and all the treasure laid up in Heaven, and Hell and the kingdom of the other world. "Fear of the Lord is the beginning of wisdom" (Proverbs 1:7).

86. Let us then implant in him this wisdom and let us exercise him therein, that he may know the meaning of human desires, wealth, reputation, power, and may disdain these and strive after the highest. And let us bring words of exhortation to his mind: "My child, fear God alone and fear none other but Him."

87. By this means he will be a man of good understanding and charm; for nothing is as productive of folly as those passions. The fear of God and the power of forming such a judgment of human affairs as it behooves us to have are sufficient for wisdom. The summit of wisdom is refusal to be excited at childish things. So let him be taught to think nothing of wealth or worldly reputation or power or death or the present life on earth. So will he be sagacious. If we lead him to the bridal chamber with a training such as this, consider how great a gift he will be to the bride.

88. Let us celebrate the marriage without flutes or harp or dancing; for a groom like ours is ashamed of such absurd customs. Nay, let us invite Christ there, for the bridegroom is worthy of Him. Let us invite His disciples; all things shall be of the best for the groom. And he himself will learn to

train his own sons in this way, and they theirs in turn, and the result will be a golden cord.[46]

89. Let us teach him to attend to political affairs, such as are within his capacity and free from sin. If he serve as a soldier, let him learn to shun base gain; and so too, if he defend the cause of those who have suffered wrong, or in any other circumstance.

90. Let his mother learn to train her daughter by these precepts, to guide her away from extravagance and personal adornment and all other such vanities that are the mark of harlots.[47] Let the mother act by this ordinance at all times and guide the youth and the maiden away from luxury and drunkenness. This also contributes greatly to virtue. Young men are troubled by desire, women by love of finery and excitement. Let us therefore repress all these tendencies. Thus we shall be able to please God by rearing such athletes for Him, that we and our children may light on the blessings that are promised to them that love Him (cf. I Corinthians 2:9), by the grace and mercy of our Lord Jesus Christ, to Whom with the Father and the Holy Spirit be ascribed glory, power, and honor, now and for evermore. Amen.

NOTES

The following abbreviations are used in the Notes:

BEFAR   *Bibliothèque des écoles françaises d'Athènes et de Rome.* Paris, De Boccard.

CSEL   *Corpus scriptorum ecclesiasticorum latinorum.* Published by the Vienna Academy.

DACL   *Dictionnaire d'archéologie chrétienne et de liturgie,* ed. F. Cabrol et H. Leclerq. Paris, Letouzey et Ané.

GCS   *Die griechisch-christlichen Schriftsteller der ersten drei Jahrhunderte.* Published by the Prussian Academy.

PG   *Patrologia graeca,* ed. J. P. Migne.

PL   *Patrologia latina,* ed. J. P. Migne.

RE   *Realencyclopädie der klassischen Altertumswissenschaft,* ed. Wissowa-Kroll-Mittelhaus. Stuttgart, Metzler.

ST   *Studi e Testi.* Published by the Biblioteca Apostolica Vaticana.

NOTES TO CHAPTER I

1. See R. Devreesse, *Essai sur Théodore de Mopsueste* (*ST* 141, 1948).
2. These difficulties have been admirably discussed by Marcel Simon in the Preface to his book, *Verus Israel* (*BEFAR* 166, 1948). The book itself is a model of its kind—impeccable scholarship presented with unremitting fair-mindedness.

3. Edward Gibbon, *A Vindication, etc.* (London, 1779), 84.

4. On the instruction of devotees in small groups, cf. A. J. Festugière, *La Révélation d'Hermès Trismégiste* II (Paris, 1949), 35 ff. and his conclusions on page 50. On the results of *otium* cf. the remarks by A. D. Nock in *Gnomon* 12 (1936), 610–612.

5. Notably by A. Alföldi, *The Conversion of Constantine and Pagan Rome* (Oxford, 1948), especially 118 ff. For a recent discussion of the pagan revival in Italy after Julian the Apostate see the able article by Herbert Bloch in *Harvard Theol. Rev.* 38 (1945), 199–244.

6. Cf. P. de Labriolle, *La Réaction païenne* (Paris, 1934), 355. He gives a useful list of the Latin authors in question.

7. From Theodore of Mopsuestia's address to baptismal candidates. See A. Mingana, *Woodbrooke Studies* VI (Cambridge, Eng., 1933), 41–43.

8. In general, see the material collected by J. Geffcken in his book, *Der Ausgang des griechisch-römischen Heidentums* (Heidelberg, 1929), 178 ff. and 305 ff. For Christian writers of the sixth century, cf. Caesarius of Arles, *Sermones,* ed. Morin, xiii (pp. 62–67), xix (pp. 86–87), liv (pp. 225–230), lix (p. 248); also Martin of Braga, *De correctione rusticorum,* in *Martini Bracarensis opera omnia,* ed. C. W. Barlow (New Haven, 1950).

9. See Appendix, pages 87–88.

10. *Codex Theodosianus* ii, 8, 20; ii, 8, 23; xv, 5, 5.

11. See page 29.

12. Caesarius, *Sermones* vi (p. 33) and viii (p. 42).

13. Eusebius, *De martyr. Palest.* 4 (*GCS:* Eusebius II, 912, 8–11). The variant version given by Schwartz at the foot of the same page states that the parents came from Lycia.

14. Cf. R. Cagnat, "Les Bibliothèques municipales dans l'empire romain" in *Mémoires de l'académie des inscriptions et belles lettres* 38 (1909), 1 ff. In the Greek-speaking East many of these libraries go back to Hellenistic times, and additions can now be made to Cagnat's list. For a reconstruction of the fine library at Timgad in North Africa see H. Pfeiffer in *Memoirs of the American Academy in Rome* IX (1931), 157–165.

15. Actually the competition in Lucian's *Eunuchus* is for a chair of philosophy, but the principle remains the same. As the system of higher education in all essentials remained unchanged for centuries, I have not hesitated to use evidence from the earlier empire as well as from the later.

16. The practice is attested for the second century by Philostratus and for the fourth by Eunapius and Gregory of Nazianzus. Ibsen admirably reconstructed such a situation in the first Act of *Emperor and Galilaean.*

17. Dion Chrysostom, *Orat.* 35, 8.

18. Cf. Philostratus, *Vitae* 2, 23; Aristides, ed. Keil, *Orat.* 32, 9–10, and Libanius did the same in the fourth century.

19. Libanius, *Orat.* 31, 11 ff. and, generally, H. F. Bouchery, *Themistius in Libanius' Brieven* (Ghent, 1936), section II, no. 18, with references there given.

20. Philostratus, *Vitae* 2, 33.

21. Quintilian, *Inst. orat.* 2, 1.

22. Lucian, *Lexiphanes* 22; *Rhetoron didaskalos* 17.

23. Cf. the admirable remarks in Quintilian, *op. cit.* 2, 8.

24. *Ibid.* 2, 7.

25. Cf. *Hibeh Papyri* I, 15, a very early example; *Oxyrhynchus Papyri* VI, 858.

26. Libanius, *Decl.* 9 and 10. His eleventh Declamation is of the pathetic type, Cimon offering himself for execution or punishment in place of his father, Miltiades.

27. Julian, *Epistulae, Leges, etc.*, ed. Bidez and Cumont, 70, 29–71, 2.

28. John Skelton, *The Table-Talk of Shirley* (Edinburgh and New York, 1895), 42.

29. Libanius, *Orat.* 43, 5 and 48, 22. On the need of Latin, cf. Himerius, *Orat.* 14, 28; Libanius, *Orat.* 1, 234 and 2, 44; Gregory Thaumaturgus in *PG* 10, 234; Chrysostom in *PG* 46, 357. For Latin in Constantinople see Ludwig Hahn in *Festgabe für Martin von Schanz* (Würzburg, 1912), 173–184. The study of law and the law schools are well treated by P. Collinet, *Histoire de l'école de droit de Berytus* (Paris, 1924), and by Kübler in *RE*, s.v. *Rechtsschulen* and *Rechtsunterricht*.

30. For ephebi at philosophical lectures cf. *I.G.* II², 1006 and 1028; also 1030 and 1031, in which the restorations can be regarded as certain; *S.E.G.* I, 368 (a Peripatetic teaching at Samos). For Cicero's studies in Greece cf. *De oratore* 1, 219; *Brutus* 118 ff.; *De finibus* 5, 1.

31. On Panaetius consult the recent work by Modestus van Straaten, *Panétius* (Amsterdam, 1946), together with the admirable review article by L. Edelstein in *Amer. Journ. Philol.* 71 (1950), 78–83.

32. A not unimportant source for the spread of philosophical ideas was the collections of philosophical tenets made by the doxographers. In time these were utilized also by Christian authors. Cf. A. D. Nock in *Vigiliae Christianae* IV (1950), 130.

33. See the recent book, *Fatalisme et liberté dans l'antiquité grecque* (Louvain, 1945) by Dom David Amand. He traces the survival of these Carneadic views, as well as some other doctrines taught by pagan philosophers, in Greek Christian writers from the second to the early fifth century.

34. Cf. E. R. Dodds, "Theurgy and Its Relation to Neoplatonism" in *Journ. Rom. Stud.* 37 (1947), 55–69.

NOTES TO CHAPTER II

1. See E. Peterson in *ST* 121 (1946), 355–372; but E. Bickerman in *Harvard Theol. Rev.* 42 (1949), 109 ff., would rehabilitate the traditional view that the name *Christianus* originated with the Antiochene Christians themselves.

2. Epictetus 2, 9, 19–20; 4, 7, 6; Aristides, *Apology* 14; *Martyrdom of Polycarp* 13 and 17; *Epistle to Diognetus* 3 and 4.

3. Gregory Dix in *The Apostolic Ministry,* ed. Kenneth E. Kirk (London, 1946), 228.

4. Marcel Simon, *Verus Israel,* 91.

5. Aristides, *Apology* 15. Similarly, Shepherd of Hermas, *Simil.* 5, 3, 7, who specifically mentions widows and orphans. For the regular fast days see page 139.

6. See the remarkable list in *Didascalia Apostolorum,* ed. R. H. Connolly (Oxford, 1929), 158.

7. Cf. Lactantius, *Inst.* 5, 1. The date at which the earliest Latin version of any part of the New Testament was made is very uncertain, but at least the Gospels seem to have been translated by A.D. 150. No extant manuscript containing any portion of the *Vetus latina* is older than the fourth century, but there are many quotations in Latin writers from Tertullian on.

8. See the excellent articles by Christine Mohrmann in *ST* 121 (1946), 437–466 and in *Vigiliae Christianae* 3 (1949), 67–106, 163–183.

9. Cf. the evidence conveniently assembled by Leclercq in *DACL* I, 80. Cyprian (*Epist.* 81, 1) states that in 258 the government proceeded not only against clerics but against Christian members of the senatorial and equestrian classes and officials.

10. *Didascalia* 31: "Sit igitur, si possibile est, ad omnia eruditus; et si sine litteris est, sed notitiam habens verbi divini et stabilis aetate." Cf. also *Apostolic Church Order* 17, 2, cited by Connolly on page 30.

11. Cyril 5, 12 (*PG* 33, 520B–521A). Gifford's translation will be found in P. Schaff and H. Wace, *Select Library of Nicene and Post-Nicene Fathers,* second series VII, 1–157. For Niceta see A. E. Burn, *Niceta of Remesiana* (Cambridge, Eng., 1905), 6–8. For repetition of prayers see Augustine, *Sermo* 59 (*PL* 38, 400): "oratio autem quam hodie accipitis tenendam, et ad octo dies reddendam . . ."

12. The Pauline authorship of this Epistle has, of course, been disputed in modern times. But its authenticity was not questioned in antiquity, and its doctrine is Pauline, not of later date.

13. Pelagius, ed. A. Souter (Cambridge, Eng., 1926), II, 380.

14. *Didache* 4, 9; cf. *Epistle of Barnabas* 19, 5.

15. II Clement 19.

16. *Apostolic Constitutions,* ed. F. X. Funk (Paderborn, 1905), 4, 11. The passage is expanded from *Didascalia Apostolorum;* cf. Connolly, *op. cit.* 193.

17. As A. D. Nock has remarked when contrasting the Pastoral Epistles with the genuine letters of St. Paul: "They belong to a wholly other world of Christian life and thought. The Church is an organized society, which has long been such." See his *St. Paul* (London, 1938), 231–232.

18. *Didache* 1–6. The date of this document is still a matter of controversy, but B. Altaner (*ST* 121, 504) is too dogmatic when he asserts that

it is a *gesichertes Ergebniss* that the *Didache* was not composed till *circa* A.D. 150.

19. This address by Clement (*GCS:* Clemens III, 221–223), together with an English translation, will be found in Butterworth's *Clement of Alexandria* in the Loeb Classical Library.

20. R. H. Connolly, *The So-called Egyptian Church Order and Derived Documents* (Cambridge, Eng., 1916), 63–64 and 181. As is now generally agreed, the Egyptian Church Order represents the teaching of Hippolytus' *Apostolic Tradition* (*circa* A.D. 215).

21. *GCS:* Origenes VI, 1, 398, 10–15 (8th Homily on Leviticus).

22. Cf. Irenaeus in *PG* 7, 784A; Tertullian, *De bapt.* 18 (*CSEL* 20, 216, 14–30); Cyprian, *Epist.* 64, 2 (*CSEL* 3, 718, 1 ff.); Gregory, *Orat.* 40, 28 (*PG* 36, 400) and also 40, 17 (381).

23. *PG* 49, 223 ff. Deathbed baptisms are also deplored in a homily doubtfully assigned to Basil the Great (*PG* 31, 424); for in an Armenian version it is attributed to Severianus of Gabala.

24. For the *taurobolium* cf. H. Dessau, *Inscriptiones latinae selectae* 4150 and 4154, where repetition of the rite is indicated. In 4152, on the other hand, note the phrase, *in aeternum renatus.* On the rite in general see A. D. Nock, *Conversion* (Oxford, 1933), 69 ff. with note on 284, and *Cambridge Ancient History* XII, 428–431.

25. *PG* 49, 234. More than a century earlier (*Didascalia,* page 39) the danger is stated more briefly: "Quoniam notum est omnibus quod, si quis peccaverit iniquum aliquid post baptismum, hic in gehenna condemnatur."

26. Cf. A. Mingana, *Woodbrooke Studies* VI, xiii, note 1.

27. See, for example, *De genesi ad litteram* 10, 13–14 (*CSEL* 28, 314, 2–4): "Ideo vivus oportet etiam infans baptizetur, ne obsit animae societas carnis peccati, qua participata fit, ut nihil possit anima infantis secundum spiritum sapere." The remarks of Jerome, *Adv. Pelag.* 3, 19 (*PL* 23, 588) are inspired by Cyprian and Augustine. In a letter written in 402–403 (*CSEL* 55, 297, 19 ff.), though he leaves the choice to the parents, he himself clearly favors baptizing young children.

28. See page 85.

29. On this whole question see Dom Puniet in *DACL* II, 2580.

30. Cyril of Jerusalem in a similar context uses the word ἰδιωτεία. Its meaning had gradually deteriorated. In pagan writers it signified anyone without special or technical knowledge of a subject and, later on, it acquired the connotation of "ignorant." But in Acts 4:13 the phrase, ὅτι ἄνθρωποι ἀγράμματοί εἰσιν καὶ ἰδιῶται (quod homines essent sine literis et idiotae *Vulgate*), means those who were untrained in rabbinical teaching; hence the rendering "ignorant" in the King James and Revised versions is misleading.

31. *De catechizandis rudibus* 15.

32. Mansi, *Concilia* II, 12–13 (Canon 42); F. X. Funk, *Const. Apost.* II, 106 and 108; I, 440–442; I, 538, 1–3.

33. Namely, the author of the pseudo-Clementine homilies (*PG* 2, 29).

34. Although F. Quatember in *Die christliche Lebenshaltung des Klemens von Alexandrien in seinem Pädagogus* (Vienna, 1946), 27, asserts categorically that Clement was ordained priest, the evidence is not conclusive; and a similar uncertainty exists about Tertullian, who certainly acted for a time as a catechist. He probably became a presbyter after he had joined the Montanists. On this cf. J. H. Waszink in his edition of *De anima* (Amsterdam, 1947), 171.

35. *Const. Apost.* I, 440 ff.

36. *CSEL* 39, 96, 18–99, 29; for the date cf. *Sacris Erudiri* I (1948), 181.

37. *PG* 33, 457A-B; 969C; cf. also, above, page 29.

38. The origin of these five "mystagogic" addresses is an old crux; for Cyril's authorship has been questioned at intervals ever since the seventeenth century. The problem has recently been reviewed afresh by W. J. Swaans in *Le Muséon* 55 (1942), 1–43. While his arguments, as he himself admits (42), are not wholly conclusive, they establish a strong presumption in favor of John of Jerusalem, who is best known as the onetime antagonist of Jerome.

39. A. Mingana, *Woodbrooke Studies* V and VI. A new edition of the Syriac text with a French translation has been brought out very recently by Raymond Tonneau and R. Devreesse (*ST* 145).

40. Mingana, *op. cit.* VI, 33–34.

41. *PG* 49, 223–240. The preacher in one of his regular sermons to a general congregation might also address a few special words to those who had been recently baptized. Cf., for instance, *PG* 51, 95–96.

42. *PG* 45, 9–106. There is an English translation by W. Moore and H. A. Wilson in the *Select Library of Nicene and Post-Nicene Fathers*, second series, V, 473–509.

43. Similarly, in a sermon on the Creed intended for catechumens, Theodore of Mopsuestia says that he is addressing his remarks both to those who were being instructed for the first time in the truth of Church doctrine and to those who wished to return to the truth after having wandered in heretical error. See H. B. Swete, *Theodore of Mopsuestia on the Minor Epistles of St. Paul* (Cambridge, Eng., 1880–82), II, Appendix A, 327. The regular inclusion by the catechists of Jews amongst the enemies of Christianity was due not so much to an abstract hatred of the people who were wrongly held responsible for the Crucifixion, as it was to the actual condition of the time. As Marcel Simon has shown (cf., for example, *Verus Israel*, 323 ff.), Jewish proselytism continued fitfully for some centuries after the Bar-Cochba rising. In addition, there were "Judaizers" among the Christians, especially in areas like Syria where so much of the population was Semitic. These facts, while they do not excuse the virulence of John Chrysostom's anti-Jewish homilies, which are a blot on his escutcheon, do to some extent account for it. His anger was directed

quite as much against Christians who attended Jewish festivals or in some
ways observed the Jewish Law, as against orthodox Jewry.

44. The juxtaposition of Jews, pagans, and heretics is made for a special
reason by Pope Damasus, who writes (*PL* 13, 364A-B): "ut credamus quia
in Patre et Filio et Spiritu Sancto solum baptizamur, non in archangelorum
nominibus aut angelorum, quomodo haeretici aut Judaei aut etiam gentiles
dementes faciunt;" but the association of Christian heresies with paganism
and Judaism had long been traditional. Cf. A. D. Nock in *Vigiliae Christianae* III (1949), 54.

45. Tertullian, *De bapt.* 1 (*CSEL* 20, 201, 4–7): "non erit otiosum
digestum illud, instruens tam eos qui cum maxime formantur, quam et illos
qui simpliciter credidisse contenti non exploratis rationibus traditionum
intemptatam probabilem fidem per imperitiam portant." The Ambrosian
authorship of a sermon on the Creed intended for initiates is doubtful. See
O. Bardenhewer, *Geschichte der altkirchlichen Literatur* III, 533–536.

46. Augustine, *Sermo* 59 (*PL* 38, 400–402); for the fragments of Niceta
see A. E. Burn, *Niceta of Remesiana*, 1 ff.

47. The Creed is explained in Libellus 5, the only one of the six that
has been preserved entire. See Burn, *op. cit.* 39 ff.

48. Jacques Zeiller, *Les Origines chrétiennes dans les provinces danub-
iennes de l'empire romain* (*BEFAR* 112, 1918), 555: "Il est de ces doc-
teurs, en accord avec le sens intime du peuple chrétien, pour qui le chris-
tianisme n'est pas un système, mais avant tout une vie."

NOTES TO CHAPTER III

1. Christian writers from the first attacked the immoral episodes in Greek
mythology. In the fourth century one may note particularly John Chrysostom's fifth homily on Titus (*PG* 62, 692–693), Lactantius, *Inst.* 1, 9–21, and
the seventh Book of Augustine's *De civitate Dei.*

2. Lactantius, *Epitome,* ed. E. H. Blakeney (London, 1950), 38.

3. *Didascalia Apostolorum* 12; similarly, Funk, *op. cit.* I, 12, 17–14, 11;
13, 25–15, 11.

4. Cf. Irenaeus in *PG* 7, 800A. Augustine (*Retract.* 1, 3), speaking of
his early treatise, *De ordine,* says: "Displicet mihi . . . quod multum
tribui liberalibus disciplinis, quas multi sancti multum nesciunt, quidam
etiam sciunt et sancti non sunt." For the need of being trained effectively
for controversy cf. the passage from Jerome cited on page 66.

5. As in the Papyrus Bouriant, of which there are some illustrations in
DACL XIII, 2, coll. 2913–2914.

6. *De spectaculis* 17 (*CSEL* 20, 19, 18–22).

7. *De idol.* 10 (*ibid.* 20, 40, 11–41, 8); *De corona* (*ibid.* 70, 168, 8–9);
De anima 2 (*ibid.* 20, 30, 20) and 20 (33, 5–7).

8. Cf. *GCS:* Epiphanius II, 523, 14–18; Lucifer in *CSEL* 14, 306, 19–28.

9. Text and translation of the *Address* will be found in the fourth volume of the *Letters of St. Basil* in the Loeb Classical Library.

10. Justin, *Apology* 1, 46; 2, 8.

11. Dom David Amand has shown (*Fatalisme et liberté*, 485 ff.) that Chrysostom's most recent biographer, Dom Chrys. Baur, has represented the saint as more favorably disposed to pagan letters and philosophy than he was.

12. PG 47, 339–340; 47, 367; 60, 225–226.

13. PG 52, 642.

14. PG 62, 291; 62, 361; 55, 316; 62, 152; 51, 274. The English derivative of the Greek word τριωβολιμαῖος is obsolete, but the *New English Dictionary* gives a number of examples of "triobolar" and "triobolary" from controversial writers of the seventeenth and eighteenth centuries. To these may be added the choice passage quoted by the late Reginald L. Hine in *The Cream of Curiosity* (London and New York, 1920), 241, note 1: "The itching of scribblers," says Howell unpleasantly, "was the scab of the time. Any triobolary Pasquiller, any sterquilinous rascal was licensed to throw dirt in the faces of sovreign princes and bishops of the Church in open printed language."

15. PG 49, 173.

16. PG 49, 121–128; 62, 472. In the passage quoted in the text I have emended the reading in Migne, ἀπονίας (laziness), which does not make sense, to ἀπονοίας (despair). Chrysostom also uses *philosophia* to signify the moral to be drawn from a Biblical story or, as we should say, its inward sense. See page 107.

17. PG 36, 508B–509A. The translation is by C. G. Browne and J. E. Swallow, with some minor changes. See *Select Library of Nicene and Post-Nicene Fathers*, second series, VII, 398. On Gregory as a classicist cf. Bernhard Wyss in *Museum Helveticum* 6 (1949–50), 177–210. Wyss deals particularly with Gregory's imitations in his own poetry of pagan poets, among whom Callimachus is the most surprising (193, with note 43).

18. For Quadratus see Eusebius, *H. E.* 4, 3 (*GCS: Eusebius II*, 302 ff.) and Jerome, *Epist.* 70, 4. One wonders whether Galen had read any of the Apologists or had met Justin in Rome. He says of the Christians that they are content with a blind faith and demand no proofs for their beliefs; but he also praises their contempt of death and their sexual purity, and says that some of their teachers are like true philosophers. Cf. Labriolle, *op. cit.* 94–97, and R. Walzer, *Galen on Jews and Christians* (Oxford, 1949), 15.

19. Eusebius, *H. E.* 4, 11, 11 (*op. cit.* 326, 4–5), remarks of Justin: καὶ γὰρ ἐπὶ τῆς Ῥώμης τὰς διατριβὰς ἐποιεῖτο. This may mean that he lectured; but it may also signify no more than that he stayed in Rome, and this is how Rufinus understood the Greek words, which he translated, "in urbe etenim Roma maxime consistebat." On Athenagoras cf. O. Bardenhewer, *Geschichte der altkirchlichen Literatur* I, 301

20. As H. I. Marrou has recently done. See his *Histoire de l'éducation*

dans l'antiquité (Paris, 1948), 432–433. He would apparently distinguish between διδασκαλεῖον τῶν ἱερῶν λόγων (Eusebius, *H. E.* 5, 10, 1) and τὸ τῆς κατηχήσεως τῶν αὐτόθι διδασκαλεῖον (*ibid.* 6, 26), but the phrases are clearly synonymous. In *H. E.* 6, 6, Eusebius, speaking of Clement's succession to Pantaenus, says of the former, τῆς κατ᾽ Ἀλεξάνδρειαν κατηχήσεως καθηγεῖτο. Marrou ignores Pantaenus and barely mentions Clement.

21. Rufinus, *H. E.* 11, 7 (*GCS:* Eusebius II, 1013, 2): "scholae ecclesiasticae doctor existeret."

22. *Paedagogus* I, vi, 26, 1 (*GCS:* Clemens I, 105, 19 ff.).

23. Cf. E. de Faye, *Clément d'Alexandrie* ² (Paris, 1906), 50 ff. and, especially, Wilhelm Bousset, *Jüdisch-christlicher Schulbetrieb in Alexandria und Rom* (Göttingen, 1915), 204, where he remarks: "So hat sich uns aus den Aeusserungen des Clemens selbst die Berechtigung zu der Annahme ergeben, dass er in seinen Schriften weithin das Lehrgut der katechetischen Schule von Alexandria weitergibt."

24. *PG* 10, 1076A; 1096A-B.

25. Cf., for example, his remarks on Epicurus' atheism in *Stromata* VI, viii, 67, 2 (*GCS:* Clemens II, 465, 24–30).

26. P. de Labriolle, *La Réaction païenne*, 243. He was, of course, thinking only of a secular government upholding ecclesiastical authority in matters of religion. But since he wrote we have seen similar suppressions by autocratic governments of books that they choose to regard as opposed, and therefore dangerous, to their officially propagated ideologies. As Theodosius I again proceeded against Porphyry's treatise, Constantine's action can have been only partly successful.

27. *Lessings Werke,* ed. Petersen and von Olshausen, 23, 156: "Um die Schriften des letztern, sagt ein Mann, der sich auf solche Dinge verstehet, gäbe itzt mancher Freund der Religion gern einen frommen Kirchenvater hin." Lessing again refers to Porphyry later in the same essay (*op. cit.* 224).

28. For Basil see P. Henry, *Les Etats du texte de Plotin* (Paris, 1938), 159–160, and for Ambrose the recent article by Pierre Courcelle in *Revue de Philologie* 24 (1950), 29–56.

29. For this, the first Latin version, see G. Théry, *Etudes dionysiennes* I–II (Paris, 1932–1937). John the Scot's translation will be found in *PL* 122.

30. Ambrosiaster in *PL* 17, 255B. On the change from the Greek to the Latin canon of the mass in Rome see Theodor Klauser, "Der Uebergang der römischen Kirche von der griechischen zur lateinischen Liturgiesprache" in *ST* 121 (1946), 467–482, together with the criticisms of Christine Mohrmann in *Vigiliae Christianae* III (1949), 69–70.

31. Cf. Pierre Courcelle, *Les Lettres grecques en occident* (*BEFAR* 159), chap. ii, an exhaustive, but in some respects hypercritical, study of Jerome's Greek reading.

32. See E. H. Sutcliffe, S.J., in *Biblica* 29 (1948), 112–115.

33. Cf. Chrys. Baur, *Der heilige Joh. Chrysostomus und seine Zeit* (Munich, 1929–1930), I, 78–79, and R. Devreesse, *Essai sur Théodore de Mopsueste* 56, note 3.

34. A. S. Pease in a notable article (*Trans. Amer. Philol. Assoc.* 50, 1919, 150–167) suggested that Jerome avoided the classics for some fifteen years after his famous dream in 374–375 (cf. *Epist.* 22), but the evidence is hardly conclusive. From 375 to 382 when he was in the East Jerome was still himself a theological student and leading a severely ascetic life, and during that period he wrote very little, certainly not enough to allow a modern reader to put any reliance in statistics.

35. *Epist.* 58, 5.

36. *Epist.* 52, 3.

37. *Epist.* 133, 1–2.

38. *Tract. in psalm.* 143 (*Anecdota Maredsolana* III, 2, 285, 23–25); cf. *ibid.* 63, 25–26, "omnes vero haeretici Aristotelici et Platonici," and also 267, 20–24. Similarly, Gregory of Nyssa (*PG* 45, 265B) remarks that the impiety of the Arian Aetius had its origin in the false reasoning of Aristotle.

39. Cf. F. Cavallera, *Saint Jérome et son oeuvre* (Paris, 1922), 1, 2, 103–115.

40. *Epist.* 58 and 53. Cavallera, *op. cit.* 89–91, has proved the priority of *Epist.* 58.

41. *Epist.* 58, 11, translated by W. H. Fremantle in *Select Library of Nicene and Post-Nicene Fathers,* second series, VI, 123.

42. *Epist.* 53, 6 (*CSEL* 54, 452, 8 ff.): "quorum scientia mortalibus vel utilissima est et in tres partes scinditur— τὸ δόγμα, τὴν μέθοδον, τὴν ἐμπειρίαν."

43. *Ibid.* 53, 3 (*CSEL* 54, 447, 14–16): "sancta quippe rusticitas sibi soli prodest et, quantum aedificat ex vitae merito ecclesiam Christi, tantum nocet, si contradicentibus non resistit."

44. *Retract.* 2, 30 (*CSEL* 36, 136, 4–5) and *De doctr. Christ.* 1, 1 (*PL* 34, 19). Although Tyconius' book cannot have been composed later than 383—see F. C. Burkitt, *The Rules of Tyconius* (Cambridge, Eng., 1894), xvii–xviii—Augustine is not likely to have known it in 397; otherwise he would presumably have used it from the first.

45. Cf. my article, "The Western Church and Astrology during the Early Middle Ages" in *Harvard Theol. Rev.* 34 (1941), 251–275.

46. Burkitt, *op. cit.*, xviii.

47. This has been brought out clearly by Sister Thérèse Sullivan in her edition of the fourth Book of *De doctrina* (Catholic University of America: *Patristic Studies* XXIII [1930]), 8–13. Greatly as I admire M. H. I. Marrou's book, *Saint Augustin et la fin de la culture antique* ² (*BEFAR* 145 and 145 bis), he seems to me to exaggerate the originality of the *De doctrina christiana,* and his arguments, e.g., on pp. 380–385 and 638, note 1 (directed particularly against the late P. de Labriolle), leave me unconvinced.

48. There was a copy of *De doctrina* in England by the beginning of the

eighth century, when it was read by Bede. By 800 or soon after the book was to be found in the libraries of St. Riquier (MS Paris, B.N. 13359), St. Vandrille, Tours (MS Paris, B.N., N.A. 1595), Lyon, Cologne (MS Cologne 74), Lorsch (MS Vatican City, Pal. lat. 188), Reichenau, St. Gall, and Würzburg. Four folios from two venerable manuscripts (saec. vi [2]) survive in the Ambrosian Library at Milan (G 58 *supra* and M 77 *supra*).

NOTES TO APPENDIX

Introduction

1. There is a full description of Lesbos 42 in A. Papadopoulos Kerameus, Μαυρογορδατεῖος βιβλιοθήκη in ὁ ἐν Κωνσταντινουπόλει Ἑλληνικὸς φιλολογικὸς σύλλογος. Τόμος Ισ´. (1881–82), published in 1885 at Constantinople.

2. Fr. Schulte, S. *Joannis Chr. de inani gloria et de educandis liberis.* Programm Gaesdonk 627 (Münster i. W., 1914).

3. G. L. Keynes, *John Evelyn* (Grolier Club, New York, 1937), 58–60; W. Upcott, *The Miscellaneous Writings of John Evelyn* (London, 1825).

4. S. Haidacher, *Des hl. Johannes Chrysostomus Büchlein über Hoffart und Kindererziehung* (Freiburg i. B., 1907).

5. Quintilian, *Inst. orat.* 1, 2–3.

6. Cf. notes on paragraphs 65 and 54.

7. Max von Bonsdorff, *Zur Predigttätigkeit des Johannes Chrysostomus* (Helsingfors Dissertation, 1922), 71, note 1.

8. O. Seeck, *Geschichte des Untergangs der antiken Welt* V (Stuttgart, 1920), 300–312; E. Stein, *Geschichte des spätrömischen Reiches* I (Vienna, 1928), 357–360.

9. Cf. PG 47, 357 and 362 (the two most tyrannical passions are love of money and love of vain and empty glory); 62, 86 and 162, and elsewhere.

10. Cf. PG 62, 324 and 446.

11. PG 62, 390; cf. also 51, 240.

12. PG 62, 546–547; the words from Ephesians are quoted also in 62, 151.

13. PG 47, 370, 383, 386.

14. PG 62, 442; von Bonsdorff, *op. cit.* 100–107. There is a similar passage on Dead Sea fruit in PG 56, 288, but this homily is not genuine, being a mere cento of passages compiled from various sermons. See S. Haidacher in *Zeitschrift für katholische Theologie* 19 (1895), 387 ff.

15. PG 53, 179. The men who have spoken freely with God are the Patriarchs to whom Chrysostom refers by name in our address.

16. PG 51, 327 ff. and note on paragraph 88, below.

An Address on Vainglory and the Right Way for Parents to Bring Up Their Children

1. Vainglory as the source of corruption in contemporary society is a favorite theme of Chrysostom's. Cf. *PG* 47, 357, 400, 446; 54, 703; 59, 43, 187; and especially 62, 77–78, introduced by the simile of the burning mansion. It is also a special danger that may ensnare the priest (*De sacerdotio* 3, 9, 211). Dissension within the Church, which is as great an evil as heresy, is discussed at length in *PG* 62, 87–88.

2. Lactantius, speaking of pagan philosophers quarreling among themselves, remarks (*Epitome* 32): "discordantibus membris corpus omne philosophiae ad interitum deducitur."

3. God or Christ as master or president of the contest is a favorite metaphor in Patristic literature. Cf. Chrysostom in *PG* 50, 618–619, where Christ is contrasted with pagan givers of games who exhibit their athletes; Clement of Alexandria, *Strom.* VII, iii, 20, 3–4 (*GCS:* Clemens III, 14, 23–25) and elsewhere; Jerome, *Adv. Jovin.* 1, 12: "The Master of the Christian race offers the reward, invites candidates to the course, holds in his hand the prize of virginity, points to the fountain of purity, and cries aloud: If any man thirst, let him come unto me and drink (John 7:37)."

4. Cf. *PG* 62, 435 ff.; 52, 585 ff.

5. The Greek words are ἐπ' ἐρημίας πρὸ τοῦ τέγους. Haidacher's rendering, "vor einem Hause in der Einöde," ignores the definite article and the specialized sense of τέγος. And is not a house in the desert quite pointless?

6. Cf. *PG* 62, 442: "There are pomegranates—I mean both trees and fruit—fair to behold and filling the unwary with many hopes. Yet, if grasped in the hand, the pomegranates crumble into pieces and no fruit, but dust and ashes, are seen to be within." As the passage is introduced by a reference to a visit to Palestine, Chrysostom's description is presumably the result of autopsy. The same fruit is probably meant in Wisdom 10, 7 ("plants bearing fair fruit but coming not to ripeness"), but the earliest description appears to be in Josephus, *Bell. Jud.* 4, 484: "fruits which from their outward appearance would be thought edible, but on being plucked with the hand dissolve into smoke and ashes" (tr. by Thackeray in Loeb Classical Library, Josephus 3, 142–144). Thackeray refers to Tacitus, *Hist.* 5, 7 and to Fulcher of Chartres. But the earliest allusion in a medieval writer is in Bede's commentary on II Peter, 2:6 (12, 255, ed. Giles): "nascuntur enim poma pulcherrima, quae et edendi cupiditatem spectantibus generant. Si carpas, fatiscunt ac resolvuntur in cinerem, fumumque excitant, quasi adhuc ardeant." Bede copies Josephus but adds three graphic words of his own at the end. Scholars seem to be generally agreed that the fruit referred to is *calotropis procera* of the family Asclepiadae, called *osher* by the Arabs. It has an attractive appearance, but if pressed it bursts and leaves in the hand only the rind and fibers. Cf. Smith's *Dictionary of the*

Bible, 3447, and Murray's *Illustrated Bible Dictionary* (1901), *s.v.* Vine of Sodom. The "vine of Sodom" in Deuteronomy 32:32 must be a different plant. See also *Encyclopedia Britannica* (14th ed.), *s.v.* Asclepiadaceae.

7. Chrysostom's denunciations of the theaters and spectacles are many; cf. *PG* 54, 660; 57, 426; 62, 428. Criticism is found occasionally in pagan writers. The rhetor Aristides, *Orat.* 29 (II, 13 Keil), remarks that children are taught at home to speak modestly and to distinguish between right and wrong. Then women, children, and young people are admitted to shows where a prize is given for foul speech and scurrility. Julian prohibited pagan priests from attending the theater; cf. *Epistulae et Leges,* ed. Bidez and Cumont, 144, 17–18. His contemporary, Libanius, also disapproved of theater and circus (*Orat.* 35, 13; 36, 15; 41, 7), but it must be admitted not on moral grounds, but because they enticed young men away from their studies!

8. There is an interesting parallel to Chrysostom's description of the audience calling the giver of a show the Ocean in a papyrus of *circa* A.D. 300. See *Oxyrhynchus Papyri* I, 41 (also in A. S. Hunt and C. C. Edgar, *Select Papyri* II, no. 239 in the Loeb Classical Library). The document records a public meeting at which Dioscorus, a leading town councillor, was greeted with cries of ὠκεανέ. The editors translate this by "hail," but, especially in view of the Chrysostom passage, would not "father of bounties" be more appropriate? Libanius also alludes to the use or abuse of these public acclamations of prominent officials who care for nothing but the cheap applause of the mob (*Orat.* 45, 22); and when Tisamenus was received in silence by the audience in the theater (*Orat.* 33, 12), he resented it as a slight. Such acclamations, which had received legal sanction from Constantine (*Cod. Theod.* I, 16, 6) seem often to have been previously rehearsed and then chanted by the crowd, or else by a trained "claque." Cf. Otto Seeck in *Rheinische Museum* 73 (1920–24), 85, 101, quoting a fifth-century example in Syriac. The acclamations in the papyrus also read as if they might have been previously drilled.

9. Luxury in houses, furniture, and so on is condemned by Chrysostom again in *PG* 52, 471 and 62, 259–260. Theodore of Mopsuestia, in commenting on the words, "our necessary bread" in the Lord's prayer, would distinguish between what is necessary for our sustenance and what is superfluous. See *Woodbrooke Studies* VI, 12–13. Even pagan authors protested against accumulation of wealth for its own sake, particularly the Cynics and Stoics, like Epictetus; and, as Galen observes in *Protrepticus* 6 (I, 9 Kühn), the unhappy people who look only to their riches lose their own souls.

10. The manner in which Chrysostom throughout this section plays on the words τὸ σχῆμά μου and its cognates cannot be adequately reproduced in English. I have used the word "place" as it is employed by Adam Smith in his *Theory of Moral Sentiments,* part I, section iii, chap. 2, a passage worth comparing with Chrysostom's words: "And thus, place, that great

object which divides the wives of aldermen, is the end of half the labours of human life; and is the cause of all the tumult and bustle, all the rapine and injustice, which avarice and ambition have introduced into this world." Chrysostom elsewhere (*PG* 59, 43–44) exclaims: "If you like to ask any of your fellow-townsmen who spend lavishly, why they waste so much money and what all this expenditure means to them, the only answer that you will receive is that they do it to please the crowd."

11. The boy made to look like a girl recalls Chrysostom's biting description (*PG* 57, 426) of the fashionable young man whose appearance is highly effeminate. "He is young and wears his hair long behind. He makes his nature female in look, appearance, and dress, and so strives to step out in every way like a tender girl."

12. To deck out young girls, especially if they are marked out for a life of virginity, is condemned also by Jerome when, doubtless with I Timothy 2:10 in mind, he writes to Laeta about her little daughter's education. See *Epist.* 107, 5 (*CSEL* 55, 296, 7–9): "ne collum margaritis et auro premas, ne caput gemmis oneres, ne capillum inrufes, et ei aliquid de gehennae ignibus auspiceris."

13. Cf. page 83.

14. The metaphorical use of the word athlete is common to pagan and Christian writers. Cf. Epictetus 2, 17, 29–31 and 4, 4, 30; Ignatius, *Epist. ad Polycarpum* 2, 3; Chrysostom in *PG* 50, 619 and 625; Clement of Alexandria in *GCS:* Clemens III, 14, 23; Jerome, *Tract. de psalm.* CXXVIII (*Anecdota Maredsolana* III, 241, 22) and passages quoted in the *Thesaurus linguae latinae*, which also gives examples of *athleta* in the sense of martyr. This meaning of the Greek word is often found on Christian Greek inscriptions from Asia Minor, as has been shown by W. M. Calder in *Journ. Rom. Stud.* 10 (1920), 52 ff. Cf. also Eusebius, *H. E.* 6, 1 and Gregory of Nazianzus in *PG* 37, 1389. In medieval times *athleta* is applied to monks, as by Walahfrid Strabo, *De exordiis*, ed. A. Knöpfler, 100: "sicut tribuni militibus praeerant, ita abbates monachis, athletis spiritalibus, praeesse noscuntur."

15. That the young child is soft like wax and can be molded by his father is said by Chrysostom again in *PG* 51, 327.

16. Haidacher compares a passage on pearls in Gregory Thaumaturgus (*PG* 10, 1152), but the parallel is inexact; for Gregory alludes to a different popular belief, that the growth of pearls is favored by dew and lightning. Closer to Chrysostom's thought is the remark of the elder Pliny (*N.H.* 9, 109), "cetero in aqua mollis unio, exemptus protinus durescit." On pearls in antiquity see the exhaustive article by Rommel in *RE, s.v.* margaritai.

17. For the simile of painters and sculptors see page 82 and also *PG* 49, 235; 47, 370; 62, 151.

18. Seal of the faith: the words σφραγὶς and σφραγίζειν are employed particularly in connection with the baptismal rite; cf. II Clement 7, 6 and 8, 6; *Didascalia* (ed. Connolly), 147 and often in the *Apostolic Constitutions* (see Index in Funk's edition). It is so used also by Cyril of Jerusalem; but

in the present passage the reference is to making the sign of the Cross at all seasons, as advocated by Cyril (*PG* 33, 816A-B): "Be the Cross our seal made with boldness by our fingers on our brow, and on everything; over the bread we eat, and the cups we drink; in our comings in and goings out; before our sleep, when we lie down, and when we rise up; when we are on the way, and when we are still. . . . Despise not the seal because of the freeness of the gift; but for this rather honor thy Benefactor." This passage may have been in Chrysostom's mind when, in similar terms, he discussed (*PG* 62, 277) the words, "set upon himself the seal of the faith."

19. As Schulte has pointed out (*op. cit.* xvi), Gregory of Nyssa (*PG* 44, 151C–153A) compares the senses to the approaches to a city controlled by the city of the mind. The metaphor is found also in Hermetic literature; cf. *Poimandres* 1, 22 (A. D. Nock and A. J. Festugière, *Corpus Hermeticum* I [Paris, 1945], 14); The Divine Mind is speaking and says, "As guardian of the gates I will bar the entrance of the base and evil workings of the senses, cutting off all thoughts of them."

20. Chrysostom omits the words τῆς χρείας in the quotation from Ephesians.

21. In deprecating the use of corporal punishment, Chrysostom agrees with Quintilian and the author of the treatise, *De liberis educandis*, attributed to Plutarch, though he knew (cf. paragraph 39) that it was a normal feature of school life. Libanius seems to have accepted it as a necessary part of classroom discipline, but Himerius opposes it strongly. He criticizes (*Orat.* 15, 2) teachers who resort to blows and says of himself that he never desires to see a scowl on the faces of his flock, but wishes to handle them by kindness.

22. Chrysostom uses almost identical language in *PG* 62, 428: "Such and such a girl kissed such and such a man, and had no luck and hanged herself." Quintilian (*Inst. orat.* 1, 2, 7) reproves parents who are amused if their small children speak immodest words, "which we should not tolerate even from the lips of an Alexandrian page."

23. Chrysostom's younger contemporary, Synesius, says of children's love of stories: "It seems that the prelude to philosophy is nothing else than a curiosity about knowledge, and in children the disposition to love a story is the promise of a philosophical goal." See A. Fitzgerald, *Essays and Hymns of Synesius* (Oxford, 1930), 156.

24. Chrysostom here uses the word, περιπέτεια, the technical term for a reversal of fortune in Greek tragedy.

25. Inward sense: the Greek word is *philosophia*; cf. page 53.

26. The naming of children is another topic that was much in Chrysostom's mind; cf. *PG* 54, 452 and 642, and page 83 above. Insofar as his advice involved the giving of names from the Old Testament, it was not generally adopted in the Middle Ages. Cf. James Moffatt in Hastings' *Encyclopedia of Religion and Ethics* IX, 145–149.

27. Cf. *PG* 61, 105: "When a name has to be given to the boy, they

fail to call him after the saints. As men in olden times used first to do, they light lamps and give them names. Then they assign the same name to the child as that of the lamp which burns longest, inferring that he will live a long life." No other ancient writer appears to allude to this particular custom, but it survived in Christian form in Byzantine times. George Pachymeres relates how the emperor Andronicus Palaeologus feared for the life of a newborn child. On the advice of an experienced woman he had twelve tapers of exactly the same dimensions lighted, and to each was given the name of one of the Apostles. The candle named after Simon Peter burned longest, and so the child was called Simonis. See Pachymeres in *Corpus Scriptorum historiae byzantinae* 35, 276–277. This and other popular beliefs connected with the lighting of candles or lamps are attested elsewhere down to modern times. See Bächtold-Stäubli, *Handwörterbuch des deutschen Aberglaubens*, s.v. *Lebenslicht* and *Name*. The kindling of lights before the statues of gods or the Genius is amply attested in antiquity; see *RE*, s.v. *Namenswesen*. In common with other pagan superstitions it was forbidden by Theodosius I (*Cod. Theod.* 16, 10, 12); but a ceremony like that described by Chrysostom, if performed in the home, would be difficult to suppress by law. Lactantius remarks sarcastically of pagan worshippers (*Inst.* 6, 2, 1): "They offer rich, succulent victims to God as if he were hungry, they pour wine to him as if he were thirsty, they kindle lights to him as though he spent his time in the dark."

28. Cf. *PG* 51, 148: "Men, to honor the deceased and to console themselves, often call their children by the names of the dead, contriving through the naming of their children a consolation for the death of the departed."

29. Similarly, in his first oration on Hannah (*PG* 54, 642), Chrysostom advises that boys and youths are neither to see nor to converse with female servants. Evelyn was guilty of an amusing mistranslation here. He thought that the maid should not be allowed to come in and light the fire, when the boy was there. But the use of the passive voice (ὑπεκκαιέσθω), as well as of ὑπεκκαίειν rather than ἀνακαίειν as in *PG* 47, 520, shows that Chrysostom is employing the verb in a metaphorical sense.

30. Cf. Clement of Alexandria, *To the Newly Baptized* (Loeb Classical Library, Clement, 375): "Relax not the tension of your soul by feasting and indulgence in drink." The phrase is Stoic in origin. See H. von Arnim, *Stoicorum veterum fragmenta* II, 123, 7 ff. (Chrysippus) and also I, 128, 31 ff. (Cleanthes).

31. Here again Chrysostom's citation of Genesis 6:4 differs from the text of LXX. The change may be deliberate; for by substituting ὀλισθήσαντες for εἰσεπορεύοντο he stresses the moral lapse of the sons of God. I have translated both words in my version.

32. Fair books (βιβλίων κάλλη) may, as Haidacher supposes when he translates "Ziermalereien," mean illuminations in manuscripts. But the passage that he quotes in support (*PG* 59, 187) does not prove his point. Chrysostom there criticizes those who have fine books but who care only

for the texture of the parchment and the beauty of the letters (τὸ τῶν γραμμάτων κάλλος), not for reading them. This he calls a form of vainglory; he also mentions books written in golden letters.

33. On the bathing of the sexes cf. *Didascalia* 1, 9 (Connolly, page 26).

34. For the example of Joseph cf. *PG* 47, 438–439; 62, 524; and especially homilies 61 to 67 on Genesis in *PG* 54.

35. "With quick glances," a reminiscence of *Odyssey* 4, 150.

36. There is little point in giving references, as Schulte does, to Plato. The Platonic theory of the tripartite soul had long been a commonplace and appears frequently in Patristic literature. Cf. Clement in *GCS: Clemens* I, 236, 4–10; *GCS: Origenes* VIII, 340, 2–8; pseudo-Gregory of Nazianzus in *PG* 36, 666; Jerome in *PL* 25, 22A-B. The last three of these writers allude to the Platonic theory in their explanations of the four living creatures in Ezekiel 1:4–10. In the language of allegory man is the rational part, the lion the spirited part, and the bull the appetitive. The fourth creature is the eagle explained as the conscience. Cf. Nitzsch in *Zeitschrift für Kirchengeschichte* 18 (1898), 22–36, who proposes an interesting emendation in the text of Jerome. Nemesius (*PG* 40, 676), following Plato, remarks that the irrational part of the soul, which is obedient to reason, consists of the appetitive and the spirited, and that the appetitive can be considered under two aspects, according as it concerns pleasures or pains.

37. On the origin of slavery which is the result of human sin see also *PG* 62, 157–158.

38. The text of the passage from Job in LXX differs substantially from that in the Vulgate and the King James Version.

39. Chrysostom has the same quotation from I Timothy in mind in *PG* 62, 154: "For if a man because he has disobedient children is unworthy of the episcopal office, how much more so is he unworthy of the kingdom of Heaven."

40. "The medical guild": the Greek is ἰατρῶν παῖδες. This is a classical usage, employed also by Clement of Alexandria when he speaks of φιλοσόφων παῖδες and Στοικῶν παῖδες (*GCS: Clemens* I, 102, 2; 151, 13).

41. Similarly, in his first homily on Hannah (*PG* 54, 642), Chrysostom instructs parents to keep their boys from hearing languishing and dissolute songs, from theaters and banquets, so that they may be pure and unstained when they marry.

42. Cf. page 53.

43. The prescription of Wednesdays and Fridays as fast days appears already in the *Didache* 8, 1; cf. also *Constit. Apost.* 5, 20, 18 and 7, 23, 1, and page 27 above. Wednesday commemorated the day on which Jesus was betrayed by Judas Iscariot, Friday the Crucifixion.

44. Chrysostom frequently reprobates swearing and the taking of oaths; cf. *PG* 49, 96–97, 102, 118–120, 141–142, 144–148, 159–160, 191–195; 60, 69 ff. In Christian writers the prohibition is at least as old as Justin, *Apology* 1, 16. Cf. also Matthew 5:34–37.

45. There is a similar passage in *PG* 62, 426.

46. In *PG* 62, 390 Chrysostom says of a Christian marriage: "Let there be no noise, no turmoil. Let the bridegroom be summoned, let him receive the maiden. Let not dinners and suppers be filled with drunkenness but with spiritual joy." The simile of the chain is used also in *PG* 51, 330. Chrysostom may have borrowed it from the Neoplatonists who spoke of the golden chain of the Platonic succession. See A. Fitzgerald, *Essays and Hymns of Synesius* I, 3, quoting what Marinus in his *Life of Proclus* says of Hegias. The context makes it unlikely that Chrysostom is thinking of the golden chain in *Iliad* 8, 19 or of Plato's discussion of that passage in *Theaetetus* 153C.

47. Cf. note 12. There are further instructions to mothers on rearing their daughters in *PG* 51, 240.

INDEX